THE QUEST FOR DEMOCRATIC LAW

DEMOCRATIC LAW

The Role of Parliament in the Legislative Process

THE QUEST FOR DEMOCRATIC LAW

The Role of Parliament in the Legislative Process

John Clarke Adams

Syracuse University

THOMAS Y. CROWELL COMPANY
New York
Established 1834

Designed by Barbara Kohn Isaac

Manufactured in the United States of America

PREFACE

José Ortega y Gasset, one of the more sober pessimists of our century, has called liberal democracy (*el liberalismo*) a supreme act of generosity, the noblest appeal that has been made in all history, in that it proclaims the decision to live at peace with one's enemies, even when they are weak![1] That the West should treasure this ideal and should take pride in its partial realization is hardly debatable. No alternative political goal merits our affection or our efforts. It is among the greatest gifts we have inherited from our forefathers, the result of their idealism and their sacrifice.

Liberal democracy assigns to parliament a major role in the legislative process. It is the purpose of these chapters to examine and evaluate parliament's performance of this assignment. The term "parliament" as used herein refers to a body of men, however selected, who officially represent the people (or in some instances, as Marsilius put it, *melior pars*). Because this body normally does more than legislate and, as we shall see, it legislates only with the aid of other bodies, "parliament," in spite of its foreign connotations to the American reader, seems a more apt name for this concept than "legislature."

The first chapter deals with the historical development of the

[1] *La rebelión de las masas* (Madrid, 1930). "El liberalismo . . . es la suprema generosidad; es el derecho que la mayoría otorga a las minorías y es, portanto, el más noble grito que ha sonado en el planeta. Proclama la decisión de convivir con el enemigo, más aún, con el enemigo debil." Ch. VIII, penultimate paragraph.

idea of democratic law. The second chapter describes the historical development of parliament in three states, England, Sweden, and France, where that development appears particularly significant. The third chapter is concerned with the contribution of liberalism to liberal democracy, and the consequent development of "constitutionalism" and other devices for protecting minorities against tyrannical majorities.

The fourth chapter, by far the longest, examines the procedures that various parliaments have adopted for the performance of the legislative function and describes some of the peculiar conditions of a structural or cultural nature under which certain parliaments operate and which appear to have a significant effect on their achievement. The fifth chapter presents the criticisms of parliament's performance of the legislative function. The sixth chapter evaluates this performance and suggests the limits of parliament's abilities as a legislative body.

The method or, perhaps better, the methods used in this book for investigating the subject attempt to follow a middle ground between the fundamentalist approach of describing formal structures and procedures and the current method of quantitative analysis. The formal structure and procedures have a significant influence on political reality but they do not determine it. Thus the legalistic approach to political science is incomplete but is not mistaken. It needs to be enriched by an historian's perspective and a sociologist's insights. I have attempted to gain this perspective and these insights through an extensive reading of the works of other scholars and through observation and consideration over the last several years of the matters involved.

There is of course much the political scientist trained in mathematics could add to such a study, but the data that could be collected and analyzed would tax the most formidable computer, and the cost of processing would tax the most affluent foundation. Such a study would complement the present one. If successfully completed, it would confirm or refute the admittedly tentative findings suggested in the pages that follow. The focus of this study is on understanding, that of the other study would be on proof. There is no intention of entering into a polemic here; it is sufficient to state that by temperament and by philosophy I was led to make the choice I did as to the approach I would take.

The method of footnoting used in this volume may merit explanation. Theories and statements ascribed to authors writing in foreign languages are often translated freely in the text and then appear verbatim in the original language in the footnotes. Citations to the major classics are usually to chapter and paragraph rather than to page. In this way the curious reader may go to any edition of the original to find the passage cited and the argument preceding and following the citation.

I wish to express gratitude to the colleagues and friends past and present who have contributed to these chapters by reading them in draft, by discussing them with me, and in some instances by actually doing some of the research and drafting themselves. My dean, Stephen K. Bailey, my editor and colleague, Frank Munger, my former colleague H. Douglas Price, and my present colleague Frank Marini read the entire manuscript and gave me the benefit of their wide experience in the field. The first chapter benefited from the suggestions of my dear friend, the late Renzo Sereno, of my former colleague Professor Stuart Woolf of the University of Reading, of William C. Fleming, Professor of Fine Arts at Syracuse University, and of Gian-Paolo Biasin, Professor of Italian Literature at Cornell University. Mrs. Emmy Clubb brought her editing talents to the task of putting in order and pruning the mass of material that had assembled.

In preparing the second chapter, I sought and received aid and comfort from colleagues in history, particularly from the late A. Robert Schoyen and from C. Vincent Confer, Professors of History at Syracuse University. Much of the research for the Swedish section was done by my former student, Professor Helge Kjekshus of the University of Dar-es-Salam. Without his help the chapter would not have been written.

Another former student, Professor As'ad Rahhal of the University of Wichita, worked diligently with me on early drafts of Chapter 5. It had been my hope and expectation that Professors

Kjekshus and Rahhal's names would appear with mine on the title page of this book but circumstances prevented them from continuing with the project. Their inherent modesty, perhaps supported by the importance they attach to individual achievement, has led them to insist that this acknowledgment, repeated at the appropriate place in the text, be the limit of their formal association with this volume.

My debt to Helen Adams can be appreciated only by those who are familiar with my handwriting and with the involved and ambiguous sentences that seem my natural style of writing. She has managed to decipher the former and to help me streamline the latter.

My debt to the scholars who have preceded me is attested to by the numerous footnotes appended to these chapters.

J. C. A.

CONTENTS

1.

THE DEVELOPMENT OF THE THEORY OF POPULAR SOVEREIGNTY:

A Survey of the Path from Vox Dei to Vox Populi

The Medieval Period

In every smoothly functioning legal system, there is a justification for the law commonly believed by and mutually satisfactory to the rulers and the governed. This justification is part of the series of beliefs that constitutes the legitimating principle, the myth, the *formola politica*,[1] or the *credenda*[2] of the society in question.

In the dominant medieval thought, the law was the word of God. For St. Thomas, as for Cicero, the basic form of law was found in the reason of God, which was co terminous with God and beyond His will to change. Aquinas called this *ius aeternum*. Parts of this law were available to man, either through his reason or through divine revelation. The norms made manifest by man's reason formed the *ius naturale*, and those made manifest by

[1] Gaetano Mosca, *Teorica dei governi e regime parlamentare* (Turin, 1887), reprinted in Mosca, *Ciò che potrebbe insegnare la storia* (Milan: Giuffrè, 1958), pp. 15–328 at 53.

[2] See Charles Edward Merriam, *Political Power* (New York: McGraw-Hill Book Co., 1934), ch. 4, "The Credenda and Miranda of Power."

1

revelation formed the *ius divinum*. Aquinas recognized a fourth type of law, the *ius humanum,* the positive law of the state, which was valid only if not in conflict with the higher forms of law.[3] Cicero had been of a similar belief: he wrote that "Law is not a product of human thought, nor is it any enactment of peoples, but something eternal that rules the whole universe by its wisdom in command and prohibition. . . . Law is the primal and ultimate mind of God." [4]

Aristotle, perhaps the most nearly universally perceptive of philosophers, delved somewhat deeper when he said: "Rightly constituted laws should be the final sovereign; and personal rule, whether it be exercised by a single person or a body of persons, should be sovereign only in those matters in which law is unable, owing to the difficulty of framing general rules for all contingencies, to make an exact pronouncement." [5] By bringing personal rule into the picture, Aristotle accounted for another institution of governmental authority, the prince, who may himself be the source of law.

Medieval political theory was often concerned with the delimitation of the realms of law and of personal rule. The jurists of that age, like all jurists, had a prejudice in favor of the law, of which they were privileged interpreters.[6]

From the concept of limited monarchy under a virtually immutable law, there arose a distinction between two broad functions of government: Professor C. H. McIlwain finds these

---

[3] *Summa Theologica, Prima secundae partis quaestiones XC–XCV,* and *Secunda secundae partis quaestio XXX.* For an English translation of the essentials, see Alessandro Passerin d'Entrèves (ed.), *Aquinas: Selected Political Writings* (Oxford: Basil Blackwell, Ltd., 1959). The second reference, not found in the Passerin edition, is particularly cogent: "Et ideo si scriptura legis contineat aliquid contra ius naturale iniusta est, nec habet vim obligandi. . . . Et ideo nec tales scripturas leges dicuntur. . . . Et ideo secundam eas non est iudicandum."

[4] Marcus Tullius Cicero, *De legibus,* II, IV, 8. English translation by Clinton Walker Keyes.

[5] *Politics,* trans. Sir Ernest Barker (London: Oxford University Press, 1952), Book III, ch. XI, para. 19, p. 127.

[6] See, for example, Marsilio di Padova, "Ubi non principant leges non est politica," *Defensor pacis* (1324), Book I, sec. 9.

implicit in much medieval juristic thought, and he calls them *iurisdictio* and *gubernaculum*. The field of *iurisdictio* is that of the constitutional principles and the traditional law, by which the king himself is bound. The field of *gubernaculum* is that of executive action, where the royal prerogative is supreme. Medieval philosophers, however, had no clear perception of this dichotomy, and no system of judicial review was devised by which acts of *gubernaculum* could be held incompatible with the eternally valid principles of *iurisdictio*.[7]

The medieval predilection for a rigid hierarchic order, and the poor esteem in which democracy and discussion were held during the Middle Ages, are shown in the *Decameron* of Giovanni Boccaccio. The framework plot of this book describes the actions of ten young Florentines who retire to a country estate to escape the plague that struck Florence in 1348. There, for their mutual pleasure and benefit, they set up a sort of utopia and agree among themselves (social contract) to remain ten days enjoying their own youth and the beauties of nature, wining, dining, dancing, singing, and story telling. For the accomplishment of this purpose, they round up a supply of servants and establish a rotating monarchy in which each will be king or queen for a day. No thought of a democratic government enters their minds. Their monarch is, however, in the medieval fashion well limited by the *iurisdictio* they have all accepted, that is, by the conventional behavior of the day, plus the specific agreements as to the rotating monarchy and the activities to be pursued. Yet in the realm of *gubernaculum*, the king's every command was to be met with unquestioning obedience by his companions and his servants alike. The king could and did determine by royal fiat the orders of the day, down to the minutest detail. He could punish the servants and presumably his companions for any infractions of his commands; but he could not order his subjects to go on a crusade to the Holy Land or even extend his rule to the following day.

Thus, in the Middle Ages, man tended to view the law (as

---

[7] See Charles Howard McIlwain, *Constitutionalism Ancient and Modern* (Ithaca, N.Y.: Cornell University Press, 1940), chs. 4 and 5.

distinct from the royal command [executive order]) as given and immutable, to which not only he but his masters as well were obliged to accommodate themselves. This concept of law is essentially conservative. Law is equated with custom, and the changes that take place are the gradual, almost imperceptible mutations of tradition. Such dependence on the law may be motivated less by man's satisfaction with it than by his fear of the alternatives. However imperfect the law may be, however far from realizing his ideal of justice, it is considered preferable to subjection to the caprice, cupidity, and cruelty of arbitrary rulers.

The rulers in the Middle Ages also tended to submit to the law, in part because they too believed the law immutable and in part because they deemed that the rights, privileges, and powers the law bestowed on them more than compensated for the limitations it imposed on their freedom of action. Thus, observance of the law appeared advantageous to both rulers and governed. The injustices that occurred were not attributed to any inadequacy of the law, but rather to some aberration in applying it, for the law was conceived of as emanating from a divine source and the rulers were relegated to the position of its servants rather than its masters. In this way, the traditional order and its basic rules were supported by an unassailable authority.

Nor were the kings under this system the sole guardians of the law, for some of the rights, privileges, and powers that the law created belonged to the people. Thus, although the medieval parliaments exercised little or no legislative power in theory or in practice, they availed themselves of the law to justify their resistance to the allegedly illegal actions of a king, some of the political philosophers of the late Middle Ages even going so far as to consider the king bound not only by the traditional law but by the reforms agreed to with parliament.[8]

[8] See Antonio Marongiù, *Il parlamento in Italia nel medio evo e nell'età moderna* (Milan: Giuffrè, 1962), pp. 546–556. Professor Marongiù attributes this position to William of Occam (*Dialogo de potestate imperiali et populi*), Nicholas of Cusa (*De concordantia catholica*), Tomás Mieres (*Apparatus*

The essence of the medieval system, then, was a government of law, but of an essentially immutable law that could function efficiently only within a conservative, backward-looking, and relatively static social system. With the advent of the Renaissance, these conditions no longer pertained.

The Renaissance

The Renaissance was a period of experiment and innovation. The new facts of life required a new constitutional setting. The same allegedly immutable law that in the Middle Ages had been protective armor now became a straitjacket that not only failed to protect, but tended to render helpless those who were bound by it.[9]

In dynamic periods of history, when the traditional system gives way to one more suitable to the new conditions, it is rarely possible to find a Solon or a committee of Solons to write a new constitution that will bring about, after a brief interlude, another period of stability. In such times, man loses confidence in the security afforded by a rigid inflexible order and seeks his security instead in leadership. The jural relation of power and liability, therefore, rather than that of rights and obligations—the leader rather than the norm—becomes the fons of the legal system. The people turn to the Tudors, the Stuarts, the Valois, the Bourbons, and to the Italian *principi* (princes, in Machiavelli's sense) for guidance and protection. Machiavelli perhaps more

---

super Constitutiones Cathalaniae), and Pedro Juan Belluga *(Speculum principans).*

[9] A. D. Lindsay in *The Modern Democratic State* (London: Oxford University Press, 1943) puts it this way: "The restraints that are built up to protect the weak against the interventions of arbitrary force become in changing times bulwarks which protect vested interests against reform. When that happens, the common man's feelings about both constitutional safeguards and absolute government show surprising changes" (p. 69).

clearly than any of his contemporaries expressed the view that rather than a conservative government of laws, the dynamic era in which he lived required leaders, unhampered in their power of action by traditional legal and moral codes. He pictured the state as the creature of the prince, who held power by means of *virtù* (a combination of ability and courage) and fortune.[10]

Like all social revolutions, the Renaissance brought a new questioning of the claims to authority of all traditional institutions—in this case, principally feudalism and the Roman Catholic Church. Although the wording is obviously anachronistic, the new spirit might be succinctly described by the expression: "I can get it for you wholesale." The rising bourgeoisie—impatient with feudal concepts and feudal structures that afforded it little protection and no status, and in the knowledge of the power its money brought—preferred to make deals directly with the king. As the outcast proletariat of the feudal system, the bourgeoisie had nothing to lose by this method, and in weakening the aristocracy there was considerable potential gain. The same class learned through the Reformation how much cheaper and more generally satisfactory it was to bypass the priests and deal directly with God.

Another aspect of the Renaissance that is pertinent to the development of democracy is the change in the direction of man's sights from the past to the future, from the Golden Age and the Garden of Eden to a better future world that would be man-made. As Professor Eugenio Garin says: "The distance between the Middle Ages and the new era is that which separates a closed, static, timeless, immovable universe, without history or possibility of change, and an infinite open universe capable

---

[10] *Il principe*, 1513. Alfred Fabre-Luce, playing *advocatus diaboli* for Charles de Gaulle, expresses the doctrine dominant in the Renaissance in this way: "Dans le temps de confusion, seule la direction d'un individu, d'un homme de chair et d'os, rend courage aux esprits desorientés. Elle imprime aux événements une marque distinctive qu'ils peuvent suivre comme un fil d'Ariane à travers l'obscur labyrinthe des événements. La personalization du pouvoir n'est pas alors, comme on feint de le croire, un facteur d'asservissement mais un facteur de libération"—*Haute cour* (Lausanne: J.F.G., 1962), p. 240.

of every development." [11] For the medieval man, the desiderata were in the past and could best be approximated by conservatism; the man of the Renaissance by contrast was critical and forward-looking, and for him reasoned innovation was almost a moral imperative.

The political forms devised by the Renaissance to cope with the new conditions were the city states of Italy and the nation states of France, England, and Spain. The major political doctrines that supported the new institutions were those of sovereignty and of the divine right of kings. Each of these doctrines held that the legitimate head of the state was the source of law.

The concept of sovereignty, which played a minor role in earlier political thought, was reaffirmed for the Renaissance by Jean Bodin, who called it *maiestas* and defined it as "supreme power over subjects unrestrained by law." [12] Bodin was a trained jurist and a public servant in the employ of Henri III; thus he was both a scholar and a practitioner of law. He witnessed the disfunctioning of medieval concepts and institutions in the Renaissance world, and he attempted to establish a political theory adequate to modern needs, buttressed by the arguments his considerable historical and juristic erudition made available to him. His major contribution to political philosophy was not the concept of sovereignty, but rather the attribution of sovereignty to a particular institution.

In sixteenth-century France, amid the religious animosities and conflicting class interests that threatened to destroy society, Bodin discovered one emerging institution that he believed

[11] Eugenio Garin, "Magia e astrologia nel rinascimento," in Garin, *Medioevo e rinascimento* (Bari: Laterza, 1961), pp. 150–168 at 158. "La distanza fra medioevo ed età nuova è la distanza medesima che corre fra un universo chiuso, astorico, atemporale, immoto, senza possibilità, definito, ed un universo infinito, aperto, tutto possibilità." See also Garin's essays, "La crisi del pensiero medioevale," "Interpretazioni del rinascimento," and "La storia nel pensiero del rinascimento," in *ibid.*, pp. 13–47, 90–107, 192–210. Federigo Chabod, *Storia dell' idea dell' Europa* (Bari: Laterza, 1961), pp. 61–65, makes the same distinction but places the turning point somewhat later, in the sixteenth century.

[12] *De republica*, Book I, ch. 8, "summus in cives ac subditos legibusque soluta potestas."

worthy of his confidence. It was no longer possible to turn to
Pope, emperor, or medieval law for guidance; Bodin's solution
was to exalt the nation state, and to bestow sovereignty on its
representative, the monarch (*princeps*).

The sovereignty that Bodin and his followers espoused was not
intended to be the oppressive force that one would suppose it to
be from merely looking at its definition. Bodin was a lawyer; he
wanted some sort of absolute by which to justify a system of positive law. Like John Austin after him, he seized on the concept of
sovereignty as the one best suited to his purpose. The sovereignty
of the Bodin school, however, was little more than the *gubernaculum* of medieval practice, a *gubernaculum* proudly asserting
its absolutism within the boundaries of its authority but thor-
oughly respectful of the *iurisdictio* represented by divine law,
natural justice, and the constitution.[13] As the decades passed,
however, and the French monarchy became stronger, the tendency
was toward lessening the restrictions on sovereignty. Thus, by
1632, Cardin Le Bret held that the sovereign had the right to
complete obedience to any command. The only limitations on
this power were the supernatural one of being morally bound to
God's law and the teleological one of commanding only in the
furtherance of the general welfare. There is no right on the part
of the subjects to disobey harmful or immoral commands.[14]

[13] A description of this emasculated sovereignty is found in Charles Loyseau,
Traité des seigneuries (1608), Chapter II, paragraph 9: "La souveraineté consiste en puissance absolue, c'est-à-dire parfaicte et entier de tout poinct. . . .
Et comme la couronne ne peut être si son cercle n'est entier, aussi la souveraineté n'est point, si quelque chose y defaut. . . . Toutefois, comme il n'y a
que Dieu qui soit tout puissant et que la puissance des hommes ne peut être
absolue tout à fait, il y a trois sortes de lois qui bornent la puissance du
Souverain, sans intéresser la Souveraineté. A savoir, les lois de Dieu pour ce
que le Prince n'est pas moins souverain pour être sujet à Dieu; les règles de la
justice naturelles et non positives, parce que c'est le propre de la souveraineté
publique d'être exercée par justice et pas à discrétion: et finalement les lois
fondamentales de l'État pour ce que le Prince doit user de Sa souveraineté
selon sa propre nature en la forme et aux conditions qu'elle est établie." Cited
in Salvo Mastellone, "Introduzione al pensiero politico di Charles Loyseau,"
Critica storica, IV (1965).

[14] Le royauté [est] une suprême puissance, déférée à un seul, qui luy donne
le droit de commander absolument, et qui n'a pour bout que le repos et l'u-

Sovereignty unrestricted by *iurisdictio* was expounded by Thomas Hobbes in 1651. He based authority not on God but on a contract, in which to escape the horrors of an anarchic state of nature, free men transferred all their authority to a monarch or corporation that was empowered to rule arbitrarily. Hobbes argues that, as a result of agreeing to this contract, every man is responsible for all the acts and judgments of the sovereign and that therefore "it follows, that whatsoever he doth, it can be no injury to any of his Subjects; nor ought he to be by any of them accused of Injustice. For he that doth any thing by authority from another, doth therein no injury to him by whose authority he acted." [15]

According to John Figgis, the theory of the divine right of kings consists of the following propositions: (1) monarchy is a divinely ordained institution; (2) hereditary right is indefeasible; (3) kings are accountable only to God; and (4) nonresistance and passive obedience are commands of God to man.[16] None of these propositions was new to the Renaissance, but each took on a new meaning and in this way formed a new *formola politica* or

___

tilité publique. Jugeant par là que deux choses sont necessaires pour l'establissement d'une Royauté légitime: l'une l'authorité souveraine pour se faire obeyr par les peuples que luy sont sousmis: l'autre qu'elle se doit proposer pour sa fin principale de procurer par toutes sortes de moyens le bien de ses sujets. . . . Le principal office du Prince est de se despouiller se ses propres intérets, retrancher de ses plaisirs, se dérober à soy-mesme, pour se donner entièrement au public." Cardin Le Bret, *De la Souveraineté du Roy,* 1, 1, 1, and 3.

See also Vittor Lo Comparato, *Cardin Le Bret* (Florence: Casa Editrice Leo S. Olschki, 1969), speaking of France and using the McIlwain terminology: "While in the sixteenth century *gubernaculum* and *iurisdictio* were still in equilibrium at least in the sense that the king granted a voice in legislation to the *parlements* and the *États généraux*, in Le Bret the balance has swung far over to the side of *gubernaculum*." (p. 138) (Mentre nel pensiero cinquecentesco il *gubernaculum* e la *iurisdictio* erano ancora in equilibrio, almeno nel senso che il re accettava, nel creare e nel modificare la legislazione, il concorso di altre forze costituzionali come i parlamenti et gli Stati, in Le Bret l'equilibrio pare spezzato tutto in favore del sovrano.)

[15] *Leviathan,* Part II, ch. 18.

[16] John Neville Figgis, *The Theory of the Divine Right of Kings* (Cambridge: Cambridge University Press, 1896), ch. 1, para. 4.

credendum which was to be paramount in European political thought for a century or so, and which marked a significant step in the development of liberal democratic theory.

To take Figgis's tenets in order: That monarchy is a divinely ordained institution was a fundamental belief of the Middle Ages. It is the basis, for instance, of the *De monarchia* (1312–13) of Dante Alighieri (1265–1321). Under feudalism, however, the monarchy was a highly structured hierarchy and the king of kings who sat at the top of the hierarchy was more a symbol than a possessor of actual power.[17] The proposition that hereditary right is indefeasible was less well established in medieval theory, since the emperor himself was elected. Yet this proposition took hold of the popular fancy in both England and France; the Wars of the Roses were fought under the principle, as were the Anglo-French wars. By the time of the Renaissance, kings of England and France ascended the throne without papal sanction, and they were enabled to do this in good part because their major claim to the throne, their birthright, received the positive sanction of public opinion in these countries.[18]

[17] See Edouard Bertrand de Jouvenel des Ursins, *De la souveraineté* (Paris: Librairie de Medicis, 1956), p. 220. "Concentrer toute la substance de l'autorité dans le commandement supérieur était une tâche herculéenne. Les empereurs ne l'ont pas réussie. L'empereur était reconnu comme le suzerain des suzerains, le seigneur des seigneurs, et si l'on veut le roi des rois, ce qui sonne comme un superlatif, mais ne l'est pas en effet, impliquant que l'on commande à ceux qui peuvent le plus aisément désobéir, et qui bientôt se déclareront chacun, à commencer par le roi de France et le roi d'Angleterre, 'empereur en son royaume.'

"Ce sont ces 'petits empereurs' qui mèneront à bien la monopolisation de l'autorité."

[18] The statute recognizing the right of James I to the English throne is, in the words of Figgis, "saturated with the notion of inherent birthright and knows of no other title." It reads as follows: "A most joyful and just recognition of the immediate, lawful, and undoubted succession of descent and right of the Crown.

"We (being bounden thereunto both by the laws of God and man) do recognise and acknowledge (and thereby express our unspeakable joys), that immediately upon the dissolution and decease of Elizabeth . . . the imperial crown of the realm of England . . . did, by inherent birthright and lawful and undoubted succession descend and come to your most excellent majesty,

The proposition that kings are not accountable to the Pope was basic to Ghibelline thought. It permeates the writing of Marsilio di Padova. In the *De monarchia,* Dante argues that the emperor is independent of the Pope and is responsible directly to God.[19] The doctrine of nonresistance and passive obedience is based on the proposition that the social hierarchy from the king down is divinely ordained and that it is the duty of every subject to obey all commands of his master not contrary to the command of God; if the master orders something contrary to God's command, the subject must neither obey nor resist his master but suffer passively whatever punishment the master may impose.

Although this doctrine is repugnant to modern thought, in which obedience is not normally rated as a major virtue, it held a prominent place until quite modern times in both the behavior and the philosophy of the western world. In spite of the fact that the doctrine may seem abhorrent to people today, it would seem hard to demonstrate that it interfered more with the de-

---

as being lineally, justly, and lawfully next and sole heir of the blood royal of this realm as is aforesaid"—cited in Figgis, *op. cit.,* pp. 269-270.

[19] See particularly Book III, sec. XVI. Here Dante establishes a dichotomy between man's corporal (corruptible) and spiritual (incorruptible) nature, and gives the governance of the former to the emperor and of the latter to the Pope. Man's nature therefore leads him to seek two ends: the good life on earth ("[Beatitudo] huius vite, que in operatione proprie virtutis consistit et per terrestrem paradisum figuratur") and in the hereafter ("[Beatitudo] vite eterne, que consistit in fruitione divini aspectus ad quam propria virtus ascendere non potest, nisi lumine divino adiuta, que per paradisum celestem intelligi datur"). Different means are needed to attain these two goals; the first we reach through philosophy, the second through faith. ("Ad primam per phylosophica documenta venimus . . . ad secundam . . . per documenta spiritualia que humanam rationem transcendunt.") Dante even turns the election of the emperor into an argument for his direct responsibility to God, while still using it as an argument for his independence from the papacy. (". . . solus eligit Deus, solus ipse confirmat, cum superiorem non habeat. Ex quo haberi potest ulterius quod nec isti qui nunc, nec alii cuiuscumque modi dicti fuerunt electores, sic dicendi sunt: quin potius denuntiatores divine providentie sunt habendi . . . ergo patet quod auctoritas temporalis Monarche sine ullo medio in ipsum de Fonte universalis auctoritatis descendit.")

velopment of the human personality than does the approved modern notion of imposing an inner conformity through conditioning.

The Christian inspiration of this doctrine is obvious, for this was the attitude that Jesus took toward his own crucifixion and it was the approved policy for Christian martyrs. The moral justification of this doctrine, which requires the subject to submit to the insolence, stupidity, lust, and caprice of his sovereign, was—according to Calvin—that an "unjust ruler fulfills the purposes of God by punishing the people for their sins." [20] Hobbes went so far as to commend passive obedience to the Christian who became the slave of an infidel.[21]

It was not only the theorists and the kings they might seek to flatter, however, who professed such a doctrine. At times, the people forced to submit to the arbitrary authority this doctrine established made voluntary obeisance before it. Thus, in France in 1614, the Third Estate proposed a motion for adoption by the États généraux to the effect that the king is sovereign within his state and has his crown directly from God; there is no spiritual or temporal power whatsoever that can free his subjects from the duty of obeying him.[22]

The concept of law as described above differs to a significant degree from that dominant in the Middle Ages. In place of an infinitely valid law of divine origin, which was as much above the king as it was above all other members of the feudal hierarchy he headed, there was established by the end of the Ren-

---

[20] Cited in G. P. Gooch, *English Democratic Ideas in the Seventeenth Century* (1898) (New York: Harper & Row, 1959), p. 4.

[21] *Leviathan*, Part III, ch. 43.

[22] Cited in Salvo Mastellone, *La reggenza di Maria de' Medici* (Florence: Casa editrice O. d'Anna, 1962), pp. 236–237. ". . . le Roy sera très humblement supplié de declarer que comme il est recogneu souverain en son estat, ne tenant sa couronne immediatement que de Dieu, il n'ya a puissance en terre quelle qu'elle soit, spirituelle ou temporelle, qui ait droit sur son Royaume ny qui puisse legitimement deslier et dispenser sus subjects de la fidelité et obéisance qu'ils luy doibvent pour quelque cause, pretexte et occasion que ce soit, que cette maxime comme conforme à la parolle de Dieu et establissement de cet Estat sera tenue pour ley fondamentable et inviolable en son Royaume . . ."

aissance a man-made law that was divinely sanctioned. While the medieval monarch was under the law, the Renaissance sovereign was its source. To the medieval theorists, including even St. Thomas and continuing through the monarchomachs of the early Renaissance, the commands of the kings were not *ipso facto* lawful. There was no moral obligation to obey the king; in fact, there might be a specific moral obligation not to obey whenever the king acted *ultra vires*. On the other hand, the Renaissance absolutists held with Hobbes that *Auctoritas non veritas fecit legem,* which can very nearly be translated, "Might makes right."

In espousing the sovereignty of the state and the divine right of rulers, the Renaissance was actually advancing democracy, for absolutism was not in fact despotism.[23] At most, it freed the monarch from legal restrictions; it did not relieve him of ethical or religious obligations and it did not emasculate the forces operating within society. Most advocates of absolutism, Hobbes excepted, placed legal limitations on the sovereign in the form of a common law or a constitution. The expression of the doctrine in absolute terms was perhaps little more than another instance of the hyperbolic language of adulation addressed in that era to persons in authority.

Many political theorists of the Renaissance—prominent among them, men with practical experience in government—were not unaware of the *de facto* role of the people in government. Machiavelli, although uninterested in the adaptation of parliamentary institutions to Renaissance politics, observed in his *Principe* (1513) that a ruler must retain the good will of the people and make them aware of his usefulness to them at all times, else he cannot rely on them in an emergency.[24]

Bodin, who had been an influential member of the États

<hr />

[23] See Fritz Hartung and Roland Mausnier, "Quelques problèmes concernant la monarchie absolue," in *Relazione del X Congresso internazionale di scienze storiche,* Vol. IV, *Storia moderna* (Florence: Sansoni, 1955), pp. 1–55.

[24] " . . . E però un principe savio deve pensare un modo per il quale i suoi cittadini sempre ed in ogni modo e qualità di tempo abbiano bisogno dello Stato di lui e sempre poi gli saranno fedeli," ch. IX.

généraux that met at Blois in 1576, sustained the usefulness of this method of consulting the people, as did Barclay.[25] In this they were following the classic author on French constitutionalism, Claude Seyssal,[26] as well as the opinion of Catherine de Medici's adviser, Michel de l'Hôpital.[27] Their insistence on the doctrine of royal sovereignty, however, obliged them to deny other than consultative functions to these assemblies—except at times when there was no king, or when he could not act.

The doctrine of the divine right of kings was also in the long run a help to the emerging forces of democracy. In spite of its religious connotations, it was in fact eminently anti-clerical in that it justified the rejection of the doctrine of papal supremacy, which threatened the free development of the national states. It also tended to restrain royal caprice. Bossuet, one of the doctrine's authoritative exponents, while denying the propriety of any human redress against a tyrant, placed on the king because of his very independence a greater responsibility to God than any of his subjects.[28]

Thus the desire for leadership dominant in the Renaissance was not an abnegation of power or freedom on the part of the followers. Absolutism was not thought of as tyrannical, but rather as beneficial. In the words of Jouvenel, "C'est un acte libre que de suivre une autorité." [29] This doctrine therefore strengthened rather than weakened the de facto power of the people, in that

[25] Antonio Marongiù, "Monarchia assoluta e istituzioni parlamentari nella politica cinque-secentesca," Rassegna parlamentare, VI (1964), 206–295 at 207, 219, 220.

[26] La grande monarchie de France (1518).

[27] Marongiù, op. cit., p. 208.

[28] "Dieu veut donc que le peuple entende que c'est au roi à juger cas, et que s'il excède son pouvoir, il n'en doit compte qu'à lui: de sorte que le droit qu'il a n'est pas le droit de faire licitement ce qui est mauvais; mais le droit de le faire impunément à l'égard de la justice humaine; à condition d'en répondre à la justice de Dieu, à laquelle il demeure d'autant plus sujet, qu'il est plus indépendent de celle des hommes"—Jacques Bénigne Bossuet, Cinquième avertissement aux protestants, XLIV, cited from Oeuvres complètes Vol. XIII (Bar-le-duc, 1870), pp. 604–605.

[29] Op. cit., p. 49.

it helped remove obstacles in their path and made of them and their representative the major focus for the polarization of latent anti-royal forces.[30]

The Reformation

The Reformation happened when it did, not because the teaching of Luther was inherently more compelling than that of earlier reformers, but because it came at a moment when the aggressive European dynasties saw in ecclesiastical reform a means of consolidating their power and increasing their wealth, because the growing merchant and trading classes, who had no place in feudal Europe, found in it a faith more easily reconcilable with their outlook, because Europe was growing economically and politically, so fast that the old structure of society had split.[31]

The political world of the Renaissance was organized territorially. Wars were frequent, but they were normally international. Independent states were the foci of political power, and politics was a game played by the princes. The successful

[30] Jouvenel (*ibid.*, p. 248) finds that the idea that will is the source of law leads typically to democracy. "Une idée était née qui devait remplir de son désordre les siècles à venir: l'idée que le Droit procède d'une volonté qui a puissance de le fonder. Cette idée devait fatalement perdre la monarchie, car si la volonté fait le Droit, alors pourquoi la volonté d'un seul?" He sees (*ibid.*, p. 237) the first signs of political liberty in the very theory of the divine right of kings. "Louis XIV dans sa majesté n'est qu'un révolutionnaire qui a réussi: un premier Napoléon, profiteur d'un premier jacobinisme simplificateur et même terroriste. Ce jacobinisme a émancipé le Souverain, en renversant l'empire antérieur de la Loy.
"Liberté pour le Souverain, c'est la devise du XVII⁰ siècle. Cette liberté consiste pour le Souverain à n'être plus tenu par des règles: désormais il formule les règles à sa guise, et il n'importe qu'il use de cette faculté avec une grande modération: c'est trop qu'elle soit acquise en principe."

[31] C. V. Wedgewood, *William the Silent* (London: Jonathan Cape, Ltd., 1944), p. 26.

prince looked after the welfare of his people much as the successful general interested himself in the welfare of his soldiers. His power depended on their willingness to obey; but in ordinary circumstances, they had no alternative.

Just as the Renaissance had overthrown the established order of the Middle Ages, so the Reformation shattered the order of the Renaissance. Religious discord destroyed the unity of the state, and where Protestantism took hold, fratricidal strife within the society brought new institutions into being, gave new functions to old institutions, and required new political theories to explain and justify the new conditions. "The princely dynasties with their armies, their bureaucracies, and their ambassadors ceased to be the sole protagonists of European history . . . from the time that a little Frenchman *pusil et mol* [the reference is to John Calvin] taught men again to seek in their conscience an authority higher than that of any prince . . . the ancient principle of divinely constituted government and the Renaissance concept of the state as a work of art, springing from the *virtù* of the prince, were about to be overcome by the principle of government by assembly and of the control of the governors by the governed . . ."[32]

Political liberty, however, was not an immediate goal of the Reformation. Rather, it was "the residuary legatee of ecclesiastical animosities."[33] As another writer puts it, "We owe our liberty to the Reformation, not the reformers,"[34] who on the whole were a highly illiberal lot.

The most successful of the reformers, Martin Luther and John Calvin, were particularly illiberal in their outlook. Luther believed in a very limited kind of liberty and in no kind of democracy whatever. He supported the doctrine of passive obedience, and thus left the individual only the freedom to accept martyrdom. Luther's attitude toward the Peasants' Revolt was that of a reactionary for whom order is of paramount, and social

---

[32] Giorgio Spini, *Storia dell'età moderna* (Rome: Cremonese, 1960), pp. 227–229.

[33] John Neville Figgis, *Studies of Political Thought from Gerson to Grotius, 1414–1625* (Cambridge: Cambridge University Press, 1907), Lecture V, para. 3.

[34] Gooch, *op. cit.*, p. 7.

justice of secondary, importance. He held that the true Church, the only one to which the pious Christian was bound, was the Church Invisible, and he subjected the visible Church to the state. All in all, as one author puts it, he was "instrumental in destroying, not merely the fact, but even the principle of liberty, so far as individuals were concerned, throughout Germany." [35] In the Peace of Augsburg (1555), his followers carried on this illiberal tradition by approving the doctrine of *Cuius regio eius religio*, which required every subject to choose between the religion of his prince or exile.

John Calvin also professed the doctrine of passive obedience, adding the touch that injustice is not ultimately unjust since we are all sinners anyway and deserve to be punished sooner or later. Nor did he refrain from contributing to the miseries of his fellow Christians by burning those within his grasp who differed with him on points of theology.

The extremely authoritarian positions assumed by Luther and Calvin, however, had only a short-run significance outside Germany. Of far greater importance in the long run was the method they employed, a method that undermined their own and every other authoritarianism. Each was primarily an interpreter of the Bible, and each relied on reason to convert other men to his interpretation, on the grounds that it was so manifestly logical that an honest man of normal intelligence must accept it. Neither claimed to add a word to the Bible or to be a prophet, a messiah, or even a saint. The message they had for mankind was not their narrow theology and their petty intolerance, but that an ordinary man can find the true religion by reading the Bible himself and by examining his own conscience.

The position of the Calvinists was considerably more perilous than that of the Lutherans. Roman Catholicism in Germany was less fanatical than the Spanish and French varieties and in much of Germany the Lutherans were soon in a majority; and at least after the Peace of Augsburg and the Peasants' Revolt, Lutheran minorities were free to migrate. On the other hand,

[35] Figgis, *Studies of Political Thought*, Lecture II, para. 18. See also William Montgomery McGovern, *From Luther to Hitler* (Boston: Houghton Mifflin Company, 1941), pp. 30–35.

the Calvinists, except in Geneva and in Great Britain, formed precarious minorities in hostile Roman Catholic states. Calvin's political theory was preached from the strength of his position as ruler of Geneva; it would have been suicide for the Calvinist minorities elsewhere to follow that doctrine, and Calvinists on the whole were too hardheaded and too little ecstatic to seek mass martyrdom. Instead, they determined to deny the divine right of the prince, as well as his sovereignty.

The Calvinist political theory that was being molded in the sixteenth century was formed by no single theorist. It developed somewhat independently in Scotland, France, and the Netherlands, where the Calvinists were resisting persecution. Often, arguments of a purely local significance were used.[36]

Although the Reformation produced no distinguished political philosopher, and Calvinist political theory was for the most part the work of passionate and partisan pamphleteers, there arose out of the hodgepodge a fairly coherent picture, in part new, in part a reflection of medieval thinking. This position denied the possibility of a human sovereign and bestowed sovereignty on God alone; it denied any divine right on the part of the king to misgovern; it disapproved of passive obedience and proclaimed the right of resistance to a bad ruler; and it empowered representative assemblies to share authority with the other major institutions of government.

The doctrine that the prince was susceptible to popular control had a long history, although in the sixteenth century there were few places in Europe where it was politic to propound it publicly. It had a respectable medieval ancestry in the practice of electing rulers, including the emperors and the Popes. Both Thomas Aquinas[37] and Marsilius of Padua[38] approved it, and

---

[36] Thus, in 1557, with the Roman Catholic Mary Tudor, wife to Philip II of Spain, queen in London, and with the Roman Catholic Mary Stuart, wife of Francis II of France, queen of Scotland, John Knox wrote *The First Blast of the Trumpet Against the Monstrous Regiment of Women*, in which he argued that since God had placed women under a malediction and curse, they could not lawfully reign.

[37] *Summa Theologica*, Ia, IIae, 90, 3; 97, 3.

[38] *Defensor pacis* (1324), Discourse I, ch. xviii.

this is one of the few instances in which these worthy antagonists agreed. In the sixteenth century, John Knox held that "princes should be . . . compelled to reform their wicked laws." [39] And in France, early in the century, Jean de Terre Rouge wrote that "the disposition of kings and princes belongs to the people . . . for the king is not permitted to change those things which are ordinary to the public status of the realm." [40] Francis Hotman, speaking from Geneva for the Huguenots after the Massacre of St. Bartholomew's Day, sought to give historical proof that the French monarchy was traditionally elective in nature and that the king's power was limited by the États généraux.[41] Of somewhat more interest was the *Vindiciae contra tyrannos,* usually attributed to Philippe du Plessis Mornay. The *Vindiciae* (1579) seeks to establish (1) that it is immoral to obey a prince who issues an order against the law of God; (2) that in such cases there is not only a right to passive obedience but a right to resist the prince, provided resistance is expressed through the people's institutions (for example, the États généraux), and not left to the devices of individuals; and (3) that the power of the ruler is not from God but from the people, through a social contract, which when breached by the prince is no longer binding on the people. A similar position was stated in the same year by the Scot George Buchanan, a humanist long resident

[39] Cited in J. W. Allen, *A History of Political Thought in the Sixteenth Century* (London: Methuen & Co., Ltd., 1928), Part I, ch. 6, sec. 2. When, in 1550, the Lutherans of Magdeburg were briefly threatened, they also issued a tract justifying the overthrow of an ungodly power—*Niclas v. Amssdorff, et al., Bekenntnis Unterricht und Vermanung der Pfarrherrn und Prediger der Christlichen Kirchen zu Magdeburg,* discussed in Allen, *op. cit.,* Part I, ch. 6, sec. 1. The Magdeburg case was an unusual one for the Lutherans. It was soon solved and had no sequel, but it shows that when put to it the Lutherans reacted as the Calvinists did later.

[40] *Contra rebelles suorum regum,* Art 1, Concl. 24. ". . . regum & principum dispositio pertinet ad popolum . . . nam regni non licet immutare ea quae ad statum publicum regni sunt ordinaria," cited in Ralph E. Giesey, *The Juristic Basis of Dynastic Right to the French Throne* (Philadelphia, Pa.: American Philosophical Society, 1961), p. 16.

[41] *Francogallia, tractatus isagogicus de regimine regum galliae et de iure successionis* (Geneva, 1573).

in France, in his *De iure regni apud Scotos*. Buchanan goes a step further and approves of individuals who assassinate tyrants.[42]

Dutch thought was obviously influenced by the Huguenots. In his *Apology* (1580), probably composed in collaboration with du Plessis Mornay and Philippe Marnix de Sainte Aldegonde, William the Silent supports the right of a people to depose an unjust king by the example of the deposition of Pedro the Cruel in 1369, thus denying the theory of indefeasible hereditary right. And he calls the Dutch Estates the sole true repository of political authority in the United Provinces. The same theory is found in the Act of Abjuration passed in the following year by the Dutch Estates, which reads in part:

> All mankind know that a prince is appointed by God to cherish his subjects, even as a shepherd to guard his sheep. When, therefore, the prince does not fulfill his duty as protector; when he oppresses his subjects, destroys their ancient liberties, and treats them as slaves, he is to be considered, not a prince, but a tyrant. As such, the estates of the land may lawfully and reasonably depose him, and elect another in his room.[43]

The deeds of the Calvinists, however, were more important than their words. The Scottish revolt marked the first time in European history that the people, as distinct from the aristocrats, rebelled successfully against their lawful sovereign. And although the government it established was highly illiberal, the revolt awakened a then backward people to a concern with politics and a civil conscience: "In the Scottish Church assemblies pastors, lairds, and burgesses sit together . . . and learn to carry

---

[42] A little later, the Jesuit monarchomachs adopted this essentially Calvinist doctrine and approved the assassination of usurpers, tyrants, and heretical rulers. See, for example, Robert Parsons, *A Conference about the Next Succession to the Crowne of Ingland* (1594) and Juan de Mariana, *De rege et regis institutione* (1599). Filmer observed that such men "to be sure to thrust down the King below the Pope, thought it the safest course to advance the people above the King that so the papal power may more easily take place of the regal"—John Filmer, *Patriarca* (c.1640).

[43] Cited in George H. Sabine, *A History of Political Theory* (2d ed., New York: Holt, Rinehart and Winston, Inc., 1950), p. 385.

on an orderly discussion. . . . The need to understand the Book arouses in the crude Highlanders a thirst for education . . . a turbulent population of tribesmen begin to discover self-government." [44]

William the Silent's long battle to protect the Netherlands from the fanatical rage of Philip II was in fact a mighty lesson in self-government. The Estates, of whom William considered himself "serviteur et élu défendeur," [45] were taught that the sovereign power resided in them. William took no action without their counsel and approval, and he declined each of their various offers to vest supreme power in him. Thus a spirit of self-reliance and much practical experience in statesmanship were acquired by these burghers, which rendered them and their children to this day a bulwark of liberal democracy on the European continent.

In the following century, it was the turn of the English to espouse and then discard the theory of divine right. James I was its most persuasive protagonist in England, but the decapitation of his son Charles I was a mighty deed that spoke louder than his own words. Toward the close of the reign of Charles II, it was actually argued in a Whig pamphlet supporting the Duke of Monmouth's bid to succeed to the throne in place of the legitimate heir James II that: "He who has the worst title ever makes the best king, as being constrained by a gracious government to supply what he wants in title." [46]

Social Contract and Natural Law

In their struggle against an inimical state, it was necessary for the Calvinists to find a new source of law. Neither the feudal

---

[44] Spini, op. cit., p. 230.

[45] Wedgewood, op. cit., p. 139.

[46] From An Appeal from the Country to the City, read at the trial of Benjamin Harris, February 1, 1680, cited in John Dickson Carr, The Murder of Sir Edmund Godfrey (New York: Harper & Row, 1936), ch. 8.

concept of an immutable eternal law nor the Renaissance doctrine of unlimited royal sovereignty was a suitable basis for a social system that would meet their wishes and needs. Consequently, the seventeenth- and eighteenth-century theorists refurbished two concepts which did not originate in that period but which gained a prominence and general acceptance then that they had not possessed earlier. These concepts were those of the social contract and of natural law.

The social contract is useful to those who seek to justify limited government and the persistence of inalienable rights remaining in the possession of the people.[47] The social contract was thus a premise in the political philosophy of the major apologist for Dutch Calvinism, the German Calvinist Johannes Althusius. His *Politica methodice digesta* appeared in 1610 embodying this idea in a systematic treatise on government, in which among other things he assigned sovereignty as an inalienable attribute of the people and designated the prince as a mere agent of the true sovereign.

In England, the concept of the social contract was temporarily diverted from its natural function as champion of the people's rights by the brilliant and ingenious philosophizing of Thomas Hobbes in support of absolutism. With John Locke, however, the concept returned to its original position as public defender against the executive. It was based on a postulation of natural rights inherent in individuals. It was thus in direct contrast to the authoritarian principle *Auctoritas non veritas facit legem,* and reintroduced the restraint of morality on law. In his concept of the relationship between the government and the people, Locke considered the latter a trustor that empowers the government as trustee to operate in the interest of the people, who are the beneficiaries of the trust. Locke thus saw governmental power as a limited power, which can be used legitimately only when its action fosters the interests of the people and respects their innate rights.[48] He reserved to the people the right of revolution

---

[47] See Sir Ernest Barker (ed.), *Social Contract* (New York and London: Oxford University Press, 1948), introductory essay, pp. vii–xliv.

[48] *Second Treatise on Civil Government* (London, 1960), secs. 135–142.

when the government should "be so foolish or so wicked as to lay and carry on designs against the liberties and the properties of the subject." [49] Locke apparently conceived of this right as an appeal to God through trial by combat.[50]

While the British were perfecting the doctrine of the social contract and using it to justify the rights of the governed *vis-à-vis* the government, Protestant Europe was returning to another discarded medieval theory, that of natural law. The first prominent exponent of this trend was the Dutchman Hugo de Groot (Hugo Grotius) (1583–1645). In his *De iure belli ac pacis,* the bulk of which consists of citations from classical authors,[51] Grotius held that natural law is the basic criterion of all justice, among states as well as individuals. For him, law was the product of right reason. He judged the propriety or impropriety of an act by its compatibility or incompatibility with a rational nature, and determined in this way whether or not the act is forbidden or commanded by God, the author of nature and therefore of natural law.[52] Grotius's own interests were directed primarily toward international law. As a member of a small and relatively weak state, he was eager to establish the supremacy of some power other than brute force in international relations. The natural law philosophy became popular among democratic theorists, for whom the justification for the supremacy of *vox populi* could not be adequately based on mere force.

The consequent marriage of the sociological theory of social contract with the normative theory of natural law marked another turning point in the development of democratic law in

---

[49] Sec. 149.

[50] Sec. 168.

[51] It is said that these citations, which must number more than a thousand, were made from memory, since *De iure belli ac pacis* was written when Grotius was in exile in a French village with no library available to him. See Albert Lapradelle, "Emer de Vattel," in Emer de Vattel, *Le droit des gens* (Washington, D.C.: Carnegie Institution, 1916), p. xxiv.

[52] "Ius naturale est dictatum rectae rationis indicans, actui alicui, ex ejus convenientia aut disconvenientia cum ipsa natura rationali, in esse moralem turpidudinem aut necessitatem moralem, ac consequenter ab auctore naturae Deo talem actum aut votari aut praecipi"—Hugo Grotius, *De iure belli ac pacis* (1646), Book I, ch. I, para. 10.

that it brought back the concept of a law morally superior to the vagaries of human will, whether that of rulers or subjects. Once the idea of a natural law based on human reason was accepted, the doctrine of the sovereignty of the people became less ominous. The people or their representatives were no longer a beast whose every vicious outburst must be dignified by becoming a precept of law; the sovereign people were merely a mouthpiece by which divine truths once discovered could be authenticated. By this marriage, lawless democracy was converted, in Aristotle's terminology, into a democratic polity.

The political philosophy that resulted was succinctly expressed by Emer de Vattel, a somewhat superficial and today half-forgotten favorite of our Founding Fathers. He stated that man's incorporation into a civil society did not free him from the obligation to observe natural law.[53] It was on these principles that the American and French revolutions were fought, and it is hard to say of either of them whether they intended to deify Reason or the People more.

Egalitarianism

It was not important to have a clear idea of just who constituted the "people" so long as they, whoever they were, remained in a subservient position. But when the "people" were declared sovereign, as in Althusius's system, it became necessary to be more explicit.

Traditional theory and practice distinguished between the masses and their spokesmen, and were little concerned with the mode of selecting the latter, as spokesmen had little power

[53] "Les hommes étant soumis aux Loix de la Nature, & leur union en Société Civile n'aiant pû les soustraire à l'obligation d'observer ces Loix, puisque dans cette union ils ne cessent pas d'être hommes; la Nation entière, dont la Volonté commune n'est que le résultat des volontés réunies des Citoiens, demeure soumise aux Loix de la Nature, obligée à les respecter dans toutes ses démarches"—Vattel, *op. cit.*, Préliminaires, para. 5.

de iure and their *de facto* power was not based on anything so formal as a selection process. Thus Locke, even after attributing inherent inalienable natural rights to every individual, was willing to assign the representation of these rights to the undemocratically selected members of parliament. The conviction that equal representation should go with equal rights was, however, to gain ground almost inevitably. It first became practice as well as theory among dissident religious groups, particularly in England. It was they who suffered the most nearly constant oppression from the government, and who most often appealed to natural rights and to contract theories of the origin of political power and of individual reason rather than authoritative revelation. And it was they who put their democratic theories into practice in their Church government, which was based on the principles of (1) the independence of each congregation, and (2) the sovereignty of its members. The Pilgrims' compact, one of the first written constitutions, was a logical extension of such Church governments, as applied to an isolated group of settlers in the New World.[54]

The Cromwellian army was another source of similar ideas. The Levelers, representing the most radical elements of the army, were, as their name indicates, essentially egalitarian. They believed that each individual had an inherent right and obligation to take part in government and to decide his destiny freely within the rational limitations imposed by natural law.[55]

In spite of these radical expressions of egalitarianism in seventeenth-century England, however, the Glorious Revolution of 1688 and Locke's subsequently published apology seemed to satisfy the majority of the British for a century and a half, that is, until the electoral reform of 1832. Rousseau, on the other hand, was less easily satisfied. In support of egalitarianism, he conjured up one of his most insightful genies, the general will.

According to Rousseau, the *volonté générale* is the common will of the entire society. It is not the totality of selfish and conflicting individual and factional wills (which he calls *la volonté*

[54] Gooch, *op. cit.*, p. 66.
[55] *Ibid.*, pp. 173–174.

de tous)[56] but rather the expression of the common interests shown by all members of a social group, which are the *raison d'être* of the group and the source of its strength.[57] Rousseau attributes sovereignty to this common will, and holds that it is indivisible,[58] indestructible,[59] and inalienable from the people, who cannot even delegate it to their freely elected representatives.[60] Thus Rousseau denies the right of legislation to a representative assembly. It is true that he had a very restricted concept of law, which could deal only with generalities, and that he left a considerable decree power to the government. Nevertheless, he raised the undifferentiated mass of citizens to the exalted position of sovereigns and in the performance of this supreme social function made no distinctions of rank among them. For prior theorists, the good of the people or the will of the people might be supreme; but the people as a whole were expected to act through their agents, and a hierarchy was established that was not even obliged to consult directly with the masses. For Rousseau, the community was its own master.

Rousseau was thus a spokesman for the new concept of man's relation to the cosmos that was developing in the eighteenth century. Christianity had established the principle of man's

[56] "Il y a souvent bien de la différence entre la volonté de tous et la volonté générale; celle-ci ne regarde qu'à l'intérêt commun; l'autre regarde à l'intérêt privé, et n'est qu'une somme de volontés particulières"—Jean Jacques Rousseau, *Du contrat social* (1762), Book II, ch. III, para. 2.

[57] ". . . La volonté générale peut seule diriger les forces de l'état selon la fin de son institution, qui est le bien commun, car si l'opposition des intérêts particuliers a rendu nécessaire l'établissement des sociétés, c'est l'accord de ces mêmes intérêts qui l'a rendu possible"—*ibid.*, Book II, ch. I, para. 1.

[58] *Ibid.*, Book II, ch. II.

[59] *Ibid.*, Book IV, ch. I.

[60] "Je dis donc que la souveraineté, n'étant que l'exercice de la volonté générale, ne peut jamais s'aliéner, et que le souverain, qui n'est qu'un être collectif, ne peut être représenté que par lui-même . . . "—*ibid.*, Book II, ch. I, para. 2. ". . . Les lois n'étant que des actes authentiques de la volonté générale, le souverain ne sauroit agir que quand le peuple est assemblé"—*ibid.*, Book III, ch. XII, para. 1. "Toute loi que le peuple en personne n'a pas ratifiée est nulle; ce n'est point une loi"—*ibid.*, Book III, ch. XV, para. 5. ". . . à l'instant qu'un peuple se donne des représentants, il n'est plus libre; il n'est plus"—*ibid.*, Book III, ch. XV, para. 11.

equality before God, but had permitted and even favored an authoritarian hierarchy on this earth for both spiritual and temporal affairs. From this beginning, the drive for equality has continued through the ages without abatement.[61] The absolutism that followed the Renaissance brought about the leveling of the nobles to the rank of the commoners;[62] the Reformation brought about the leveling of the priests as each man assumed the right to read and interpret his Bible as he chose. The next step was to make the rulers themselves the creatures of the people. Charles I and Louis XVI lost their lives to establish this principle, and the Dutch and American revolutions were fought in its name. As man's interest turned increasingly from the spiritual to the material world and there came to him the conviction that he was master of his own destiny, even God began to lose His majesty as man became in his own mind the center of the Universe. Thus by the eighteenth century—with the discarding of *Cuius regio eius religio*, the rise of Nonconformism, and the end of the Inquisition—religious faith again became a mode of self-expression rather than a rite of submission to constituted human authority. In the world of the Industrial Revolution, God's reason was no longer a sufficient justification of the law. Theologians and priests were on the whole discredited, and God perhaps has never completely recovered from the effects of such eighteenth-century epithets as the Superintendent.[63]

[61] "Le développement graduel de l'égalité des conditions est donc un fait providentiel, il en a les principaux caractères: il est universel, il est durable, il echappe chaque jour à la puissance humaine, tous les événements, comme tous les hommes, servent à son développement." Alexis de Tocqueville, *De la démocratie en Amérique* (1835), Introduction.

[62] "En France, les rois se sont montrés les plus actifs et les plus constants des niveleurs. Quand ils ont été ambitieux et forts, ils ont travaillé à élever le peuple au niveau des nobles; et quand ils ont été modérés et faibles, ils ont permis que le peuple se plaçât au-dessus d'eux-mêmes. Les uns ont aidé la démocratie par leurs talents, les autres par leurs vices. Louis XI et Louis XIV ont pris soin de tout égaliser au-dessous du trône, et Louis XV est enfin descendu lui-même avec sa cour dans la poussière . . . " *ibid.*

[63] See, for example, David Hume, *On the Social Contract*, para. 3. "The same Divine Superintendent, who, for wise purposes, invested a Titus or

So long as the Christian doctrine of original sin dominated man's thought, it was difficult to defend the proposition that man could be master of his own and other people's destinies. In postulating the essential goodness of man, in popularizing the fantasy of the good savage, and in designating social injustice and not human nature as the source of sin, Rousseau helped clear away the basis of Christian humility. In so doing, he laid the foundation for egalitarian democracy.

The Modern Period

The nineteenth and twentieth centuries have brought refinements to liberal democracy and have witnessed its spread throughout the world. Their major contribution to the theory of democratic law has been an inclination to question the eternal validity of a static natural law, thus removing the last objective restraint on the sovereignty of the people.

In liberal democracy, law is therefore for the first time in history the servant of the people. Although the people must obey the law so long as it remains in force, it is theirs to alter when and as they will; thus the proposition has been reasserted that the law is above the rulers (but not above the people, who are its source). The pendulum, however, has not swung back to a static society where law is essentially a natural law suitable to all ages; as in the age of absolutism, law in the liberal democratic era must adapt to the needs of a rapidly changing society. As a modern judge has put it, "That law is but the tool, not the driving force, of the great society, that it must remain ever servant, never master, is a statement hardly likely to startle modern ears." [64]

---

a Trajan with authority, did also, for purposes no doubt equally wise, though unknown, bestow power on a Borgia or an Angria."

[64] Charles E. Clark, "The Function of Law in a Democratic Society," *University of Chicago Law Review*, IX (1942), 393–405 at 393.

By the end of the eighteenth century, the quest for democratic law seemed to be over, for its source had apparently been discovered. The proposition that the function of declaring the law should be entrusted to a traditional institution, one that had long been the spokesman of the people and the defender of their interests before their rulers, had already gained acceptance in what were later to become the most important western states— Great Britain, the United States, and France. Kings, priests, and judges, custom, reason, and tradition had all been demoted, and this institution, parliament, exalted in their place. And if for some, God still lurked metaphysically in the background, it was only as the source of the source of the source, for *vox dei* if heard at all was to be expressed through *vox populi,* as *vox populi* was to be expressed through parliament.

We turn next to the history of that institution to which we have entrusted the power of determining the laws that will order and control our lives.

2.

THE HISTORICAL DEVELOPMENT OF PARLIAMENT:

A Tale of Healthy Twins and a Miscarriage

Introduction

Wherever human beings are treated as men by the government, and not as mere things possessed, rulers have called the people or their representatives together from time to time for the purpose of deliberation. Such gatherings are the seeds from which parliaments grow. In only a few nations, however, has a parliamentary tradition been able to prosper through the centuries; contemporary parliaments are rarely the products of a long-standing native tradition.

The parliamentary system got its start in western Europe with the breakdown of feudalism and the rise of the cities and the bourgeoisie. Embryonic parliaments sprang up spontaneously over a period of a little more than a century in each of the major European states. The new factor in each instance was the admission of representatives of the bourgeoisie into the formerly purely feudal councils of the king.

The *cortes* of León and Castille were first called together in 1188 and 1189, respectively. In 1232, the German diet met for the first time. Since these particular attempts at the establishment of incipient parliamentary institutions were soon abandoned, we shall turn our attention here to the parliamentary institutions in Great Britain, Sweden, and France; Great Britain and Sweden because they have the longest uninterrupted parliamentary history, and France because of the length and turbulence of its parliamentary history. We shall seek the historical origins of these institutions and trace their separate developments, showing what they had in common and what differences arose among them, how experienced they became as legislative organs, and how suited they were to perform their new function as the principal source of legislative power.

The natural development of a parliamentary tradition is slow, and its fashioning is piecemeal, with no ultimate goal in mind. There is a vast difference between a consultative assembly that meets irregularly and infrequently to advise a ruler, and the modern legislative assembly of liberal democracies, which we are calling by the generic name of parliament. In its early history, this institution was bent to suit short-term purposes and was judged and justified by what it did rather than by what it might become. Therefore, the direction of its early growth was determined by the occasional ends it could be put to serve, and not by a blueprint for long-term political development. Modern conceptions of parliament grew out of the political ferment of seventeenth-century England. By that time, parliament was an integral part of the English constitution; the traditional institution was merely recast in terms of seventeenth-century theory and practice.

The British Parliament

In any society, the national will is a political force that the government dares not neglect, for where the masses will not follow the rulers cannot lead. Even as far back as the Anglo-Saxon period, the national will of the English had legal as well as political significance, based on the *promissio regis,* the royal oath that was part of the coronation ritual. Ethelred the Redeless at

his coronation in 979, for instance, swore that he would be to
his people "a mild and devoted lord" and "would consent in all
things to their will." [1] Consideration of the national will was
thus not only a question of political expediency but also a moral
obligation.

The English parliament is traced back to the Anglo-Saxon
witenagemot, a word that denoted etymologically a gathering
of wise men and realistically an assembly of the important lords
within the central administration. By the tenth century, the
witenagemot served as a sounding board and a means for publicizing the decisions made by the king and his immediate counselors. Although it might have been dangerous and certainly
was impolitic to contradict the king directly, the witenagemot
doubtless permitted the king to feel out the temper of his political adversaries. Whether or not the witenagemot was representative in the modern sense, "it was unquestionably looked
upon as representing the whole people and consequently the
national will." [2]

In the Norman period, the witenagemot was feudalized and its
name latinized to *curia regis*. The witenagemot had been composed of the high officials of state and Church and there had
been little or no obligation to attend its meetings. Similar high
officials were also members of the *curia regis* in their capacities
as feudal tenants in chief, and in this case attendance was com-
pulsory. On festive occasions, that is, at Easter, Whitsuntide, and
Christmas, when even the lesser barons were expected to be
present, the body numbered some 500. When ordinary business
was to be conducted, however, about 50 of the 170 great barons
generally attended, along with such high administrative officers
of the royal household as the chancellor, the chamberlain, the
marshal, and the constable.[3]

Legislation during the Anglo-Saxon and Norman period, and

---

[1] Cited by Bryce Lyon, *A Constitutional and Legal History of Medieval
England* (New York: Harper & Row, 1960), p. 40.

[2] Thomas Pitt Taswell-Langmead, *English Constitutional History*, 10th
ed., revised by Theodore F. T. Plunkett (Boston: Houghton Mifflin Company,
1946), p. 21.

[3] Lyon, *op. cit.*, p. 143.

on down to the fourteenth century, was an extraordinary procedure. The few laws that were promulgated were manifestations of the royal prerogative, generally without benefit of either the advice or the consent of parliament. When not being used as instruments of communication between the king and the more influential of his subjects, the witenagemot and later the *curia regis* functioned as courts of law, with primary jurisdiction in important civil and criminal cases. Thus, both were looked upon more as a body of experts competent to give an authoritative statement of the law than as a repository of either the will or the reason from which new legislation would issue.

Under the first Plantagenets (Henry II and his sons Richard and John), the crown attained its greatest power in the medieval period. Yet Henry and Richard did not neglect the council of the royal barons. Although still called *curia regis,* the council was more commonly referred to as *magna curia* or *magnum concilium,* or even a colloquium. The latter suggests that the council at least discussed the issues instead of merely assenting to the royal will. As long as the king was present, the *curia* was still only a consultative body with no right even to be consulted; but in the king's absence, it occasionally showed more initiative. These absences were frequent, as all the Plantagenets spent much time in France protecting their interests there, and Richard was crusading or imprisoned in Europe during the greater part of his reign.

The greatest single achievement in constitutional government that was accomplished in the period of the early Plantagenets was Magna Carta. It is not for the many successes of these kings but for this, their colossal failure, that the Anglo-American world today has most reason to be grateful. Magna Carta is not only the basis of the present British constitution; it marks the first instance of a typically British procedure in constitutional reform, a procedure based on compromise and consent, on the conservation of traditional institutions coupled with radical changes in the power structure, rather than on the *tabula rasa* techniques of visionaries and revolutionaries.

Many of the provisions of Magna Carta do not concern us here; they were matters of feudal practice, and the whole document was of an essentially conservative nature. The importance of Magna Carta lies in its reaffirmation of the principle of *iurisdictio,* in the limits it placed on *gubernaculum,* and in its assertion of the right to revolt should the king fail to honor his word. King John was a tyrant who did not respect the law. In submitting to the barons, led by the Archbishop of Canterbury, Stephen Langton, John in fact did obeisance before the law, and absolutism was set back. Only in this sense can Magna Carta be considered a democratic document. Its immediate purpose was to reestablish the *status quo ante* after the king started to interfere with the interests of the barons and the clergy.

John died in 1216, after repudiating Magna Carta. During the rest of the century his son Henry III, and his grandson, Edward I, frequently reaffirmed and re-repudiated the document; but on the whole, significant progress was made in establishing the feudal rights of the barons and of the emerging burgesses against the arbitrary use of the prerogative by the king.

The first citadel of royal power to be successfully assaulted was the small council, a body composed of the king's major permanent advisers, and a forerunner both of the privy council and the cabinet. Henry preferred to staff this council with his various French favorites; the English barons claimed a right as his major feudal vassals to be his major counselors. In a meeting of the *curia,* now called the great council, in 1237 they refused to grant the king money unless he replaced his present counselors with the "natural" ones, that is, the representatives of the great barons. Financial necessity forced Henry to comply with these demands; a panel of counselors acceptable to the barons swore on oath to give the king good advice and the king swore to abide by it. Henry broke his word within the year; nevertheless, an important principle in limited and representative government had been stated.

In 1244, financial necessity again compelled Henry to convene the great council. On this occasion it sought to require the king to appoint to the small council four men nominated and removable only by the great council. Perhaps to avoid a showdown, Henry quickly appointed counselors who met with baronial approval and the great council took no formal action on the matter.

In 1248, Henry faced a major crisis. In exchange for the papal grant of the throne of Sicily for his second son, Edmund, Henry had agreed to pay the papal military debt of 135,000 marks. Since he was again virtually bankrupt, he convened another great council, this time at Oxford. The barons appeared in full armor and in a belligerent mood. To meet their demands, a small council of 15 members was set up, dominated by the barons and responsible to the great council. The barons stipulated that the top administrative officials, the justiciar, the chancellor, and the treasurer, should be nominated by the great council and made responsible to the small council. Henry vowed to grant these demands, and this form of limited monarchy functioned for three years. In 1261, however, the Pope conveniently freed Henry from the obligation of honoring his oath and he was able to return to his old system of government. Effective power returned again to the barons in 1264, after the victory of the baronial forces under Simon de Montfort. When Montfort died in the following year, Henry regained some of his authority but he was careful thenceforth to choose his counselors among the barons and to consider their wishes.

During the reign of Edward I (1272–1307), the small council gradually became recognizably the forerunner of the privy council. It had a total membership of about 60 persons, but usually met in much smaller numbers. Not only representatives of the barons and the clergy but many technicians, experts, and administrative officers as well were members. Edward, who was credited with being an exceptionally able administrator, sought to get much of the routine judicial work of the great council performed by the small council. This work was essentially of a private nature and dealt with individual grievances. Edward preferred to handle these claims in a more routine and expeditious manner, so that more of the great council's time would be free for matters of public policy. At this period, the small council also took on the new function of issuing orders in council. The great reliance this king placed on the small council and its efficiency helped make it an ineradicable part of the English constitution.

The greatest constitutional achievement of thirteenth-century England, however, was the formation of parliament. "However essential were the central and local organs of government and however admirable the common law and its principles, they were but subordinate and supporting elements—the flying buttresses and columns—of the great Gothic cathedral that was parliament." [4]

Parliament was formed when the middle classes entered the great council. This metamorphosis occurred as both the kings and the barons sought new sources of support in the power struggle between them, and as the newly acquired wealth of the burgesses rendered this class a significant potential source of revenue. The advent of this group on the political scene marked a revolution in the power structure, and the death of feudalism. There was no feudal custom to determine the rights and obligations of the upstart burgesses. Indeed, feudalism scarcely recognized its weapon, monetary wealth. But the kings were ever in need of money for their wars and they had to placate the rising merchants in order to gain their financial support; it was through parliament that the king had contact with his burgesses.

The calling together of representatives of town and county to discuss local matters dates back to the reign of John. In 1227, Henry III ordered each county court to elect four "lawful and discreet knights" to meet with the great council at Westminster to air complaints against the sheriffs. In 1254, Henry summoned two knights from each county and representatives of the lesser clergy to meet with the great council. As the struggle between Henry and Simon de Montfort, Earl of Leicester, grew more intense, both sides sought the support of the middle classes. In 1265, Montfort convened a great council with burgesses to represent the boroughs. The development of parliament in the thirteenth century, however, was not a steady evolution. There were frequent false starts and almost as many steps backward as for-

[4] Lyon, *op. cit.*, p. 408.

ward. Of some 70 assemblies called parliaments convened between 1258 and 1300, only 9 followed Montfort's precedent and included representatives of both county and borough.[5]

In 1295 when war broke out virtually simultaneously in France and on the Scottish and Welsh borders, Edward convened a parliament to take unified action in a national emergency. The French appropriately emphasized the emergency by landing at Dover on the day parliament had been summoned to meet at Westminster. Edward needed money badly but he also needed a united country behind him, and in convening parliament he probably sought to gain psychological as well as economic benefits. In the summons, Edward cited a Roman dictum, *Quod omnes tangit ab omnibus approbetur,* which probably expresses as succinctly as possible the thirteenth-century thinking on parliament: Matters of public concern should be approved by the public.

This gathering is known as the "model" parliament and was once considered the first modern parliament, but recent research has discovered that it did not deviate radically from the practice of previous parliaments of the century. Its greater prestige is probably due to the crisis that occasioned its convening and to the consequent deeper realization of parliament's powers and purpose. The model parliament was probably the largest parliament so far convened and included about 100 lords spiritual, half as many great barons, 75 knights, and over 200 burgesses, as well as representatives of the lower clergy.

The division into Lords and Commons occurred in the fourteenth century. It was the medieval custom to gather together to hear the king's "speech from the throne" and then, when the king retired with his ministers, to break up into three groups. The great barons, the archbishops and bishops, and the knights all met together as one group; the lower clergy formed a second group; and the burgesses a third. Each voted its own taxes. The reason that the archbishops and bishops met with the lay barons was because of their rank as feudal tenants in chief of the king.

[5] *Ibid.,* p. 418.

Normally each group assessed itself at a different rate. It has been suggested that the division was encouraged by the kings, in pursuance of the policy, *Divide et impera*.[6]

The division into two houses instead of three as in France or four as in Sweden was in part the result of the defalcation of the lesser clergy. Although the practice of convening representatives of the knights and the burgesses in parliament soon became a constitutional convention, Edward's attempts to include representatives of the lesser clergy as well were in the long run unsuccessful. The medieval clergy were a law unto themselves and had to be treated almost as a foreign nation. Their pretensions to special treatment were buttressed by the Pope and by the religious faith and superstitious fear often present in sovereign and subjects alike. The clerics had little interest in commingling with secular parliaments and would rather deal with the king through special ecclesiastical convocations. They not only professed but possessed freedom from common law—hence the well-known abuses of benefit of clergy, as Henry I learned in his conflict with Thomas Becket. For some fifty years after the model parliament, the clergy were frequently summoned but their attendance was reluctant and intermittent; after the middle of the fourteenth century, they were no longer summoned. Their absence prevented the creation in England of a separate house of parliament representing the ecclesiastical interests, such as developed in both Sweden and France. In England, the top prelates joined the great barons in the House of Lords and the lesser clergy stayed away.

The peculiar nature of the two houses in England reflected the evolution of class interests and of the English class structure. The knights were originally attached to the great barons by feudal ties, but the barons grew bold as they struggled among themselves and against their often weak and ever needy kings. It was not to the knights' interest to play power politics for these high stakes, as they could hope to gain little personal benefit from their intervention and could easily incur utter ruin

[6] Sir Ernest Barker, *Essays on Government* (Oxford: The Clarendon Press, 1945), p. 63.

for themselves if they lacked the prescience to choose the winning side. The knights therefore gradually joined with the burgesses, with whom their economic and political interests more nearly coincided. The cutoff point between the interests, and consequently between the two houses of parliament, was maintained at a high point in the power hierarchy by the great barons' retention of the system of primogeniture, which they had inherited from feudalism. Thus the peculiar English class structure was created: a structure that for centuries was to be reflected in parliament and to mark the essential features that distinguished the English class system from that of the continent.[7]

This division of interests was also reflected in a division of functions between the two houses of parliament. The knights and burgesses reached agreement on tax limitation in 1339 and thenceforth fought for and gained the exclusive right to initiate money bills, thus establishing the power of the purse as the basis of parliamentary strength. This power derives from the feudal principle that the king cannot impose extraordinary taxes without the consent of those who must pay them. Parliament held tenaciously to this power until it was gradually lost to the cabinet and the parties over the last hundred years. The Lords, on the other hand, took over exclusively the judicial power of the small council. At first they used this power for political ends, and thus until the advent of the Lancastrian kings in 1399 the Lords dominated the political scene as well.

The legislative activity of parliament also increased in the thirteenth century. Legislation held a minor position among government activities in the Middle Ages because law was considered something given and immutable. What legislative power there was, however, was believed to emanate from the royal prerogative. Magna Carta is sometimes called England's first statute; still, it was little more than a restatement of existing law. By the end of the thirteenth century, although statutes were

---

[7] See Albert Frederick Pollard, "The Advent of the Middle Class," in Pollard, *Factors in Modern History* (New York: G. P. Putnam's Sons, 1907), pp. 26–51.

still formally an expression of the king's will, the practice of legislating in parliament (but not by parliament) began to take root. Thus Edward I "at the request of the magnates" enacted the statute of *Quia emptores*, which allowed greater freedom in the alienation of real property. Edward also issued the writ of *Quo warranto* and determined on the policy of expelling the Jews as the result of parliamentary initiative.

From a juristic point of view, the culminating achievement of the medieval parliament was the deposition of Richard II. The realists will tell us that Richard lost the throne because of his own incompetence and the military prowess of his adversary, Henry of Lancaster; but force of arms alone was not enough to legitimize Henry's seizure of the throne in the eyes of many of his subjects and perhaps in his own eyes as well. Parliament's action was Henry's justification; it legalized what otherwise Henry could have claimed only by right of conquest. The parliamentary coup of 1399 was followed quickly by other victories, for it might be said that the Lancastrian kings reigned by grace of parliament.

In 1401, parliament established the precedent of refusing to enact financial legislation until its petitions to the king had been favorably acted upon. This was exercise of the power of the purse with a vengeance. In 1414, parliament established the principle that the king must accept or reject petitions in the form he received them from parliament. If in agreement, the king appended the words *"Le roi le veut"* (according to some, *"Le roy le veult"*). On those he rejected, he wrote *"Le roi s'avisera,"* thus showing even in his refusal a deference to parliament that did not savor of an absolute sovereign.

The fifteenth century also witnessed an increased interest on the part of parliament in controlling the administration. It continued to require the king to submit sporadically to a post audit, it made nominations to the small council, and it removed administrative officers by the procedure of impeachment until the middle of the century and thereafter by bills of attainder. (Impeachment is a judicial proceeding in which the Commons are the prosecutors, supporting their accusations by evidence, and the Lords are the judges. Attainder is in the form of legislation and the procedure is that employed for any other bill; it need not be supported by evidence. Attainder was therefore more expeditious but less judicial than impeachment.) The success of parliament was due in considerable part to fortuitous circumstances. The eight kings of the Plantagenet dynasty, who ruled England from 1154 to 1399, were continually involved in the conquest, reconquest, defense, and administration of their French possessions. Only sporadically could their full attention be devoted to the governing of England. For them England was above all a source of revenue that made it possible for them to fight in France: the desire for, and often dire need of additional revenue led these kings out of prudence and necessity to consider the interests of those on whom they depended for financial support.

The more able administrators among these kings, Henry II and Edward I, encouraged the development of the great system of common law courts, which served the double function of pacifying the realm and filling the king's coffers, for even in the Middle Ages justice was costly. These kings also perfected the system of local administration, in which effective power was in good measure entrusted to local notables.

In thus building up the strength and wealth of England they helped create as a by-product the power and prestige of the class of Englishmen versed in the law, who would make good their claims to rights against the kings.

The century following the convocation of the model parliament was marked by bitter struggles between the barons and the kings. The protagonists in the struggle were lesser men than the leaders in the thirteenth century had been. Nevertheless, in spite of the greed, shortsightedness, and vindictiveness of the great barons and despite their momentarily calamitous defeats, the cause of parliament registered significant gains. The *magnum concilium* that the first Plantagenet, Henry II, had convened on ceremonial occasions in the second half of the twelfth century was sufficiently powerful 200 years later to dispossess the last of the Plantagenets, Richard II, from his throne.

Thus for two and a half centuries the strong kings found it expedient to placate the great barons, the prelates, and later the

representatives of the people; while the weak kings by their ar-
rogance and stupidity stimulated them to ever greater assertions
of power, which these kings were unable to resist.

Behind these accidents of history, however, lay still more basic
causes for the success of parliament. In the first place, as already
mentioned, social power is the result of the interaction between
leaders and followers. Leaders give orders, but if they wish to
be followed they must know the right orders to give. As Austin
said, a sovereign is only a sovereign so long as he is customarily
obeyed. To take the advice and counsel of parliament and be
swayed by its petitions is not the sign of a weak ruler. The successful leader should try to create and mold public opinion in
order better to serve the common interest; but he must also con-
stantly seek to know the public temper, for only at the risk of
his position may he run counter to it.

In the second place, power, as James Harrington tells us,
tends to follow property. An absolute monarchy presupposes
absolute control of property by the monarch. In medieval England, the great barons, the Church, and increasingly the knights
and the burgesses held property. It is an old and true maxim
that he who pays the piper calls the tune.

Still more important perhaps was the fact that parliament actually represented far more than the vested interests of reactionary and narrow-minded barons, unenlightened clergy, and
wealthy burgesses; it was also the champion of the principle of
the supremacy of law over arbitrary rule, of *iurisdictio* over *gubernaculum*. Henry de Bracton, commonly considered England's
greatest medieval jurist, held the king to be not *sub homine* but
sub legibus. The medieval parliament was only occasionally and
incidentally a lawmaking body, but it was continually and essentially the defender and the custodian of the law; thus, in its
struggle against the arbitrary use of the royal prerogative, parliament could assume a position of moral superiority.

Traditions of long standing were behind parliament's position.
The coronation oaths by which the Anglo-Saxon kings swore to
respect the law and the rights of the people were repeated and
strengthened through the centuries, and although these oaths
were often repudiated in practice, by 1399 Richard II's alleged

failure to act in accordance with his coronation oath constituted the moral and legal justification for his deposition.

The major defect in the medieval system of government lay not in the constitutional provisions and the division of power between *iurisdictio* and *gubernaculum*, but rather in the absence of an effective sanction against a king who chose to act *ultra vires*. In England, parliament gradually acquired the power and prestige to apply this sanction.

The position of parliament as defender and custodian of the law was further strengthened by its traditional activity as the king's highest court. The medieval mind did not envisage a separation of powers, and no distinction was attempted among the various functions of government. Policy formation, administration, and adjudication were intermingled in a unified concept of the process of government, and the king used the same men and the same institutions to help him perform each of these functions.

The Hundred Years' War with France and the Wars of the Roses closed England's medieval period with almost a century and a half of chaos (1337–1485). While the wars with France had tended to unite parliament against the king on fiscal policy and thus through the power of the purse to strengthen parliament's hand *vis-à-vis* the king, the Wars of the Roses divided parliament between partisans of Lancaster and York, and parliament by the use of procedures such as the bill of attainder was guilty of the same arbitrary use of power that during this period disfigured other phases of English public life.

With the advent of the Tudors in 1485, stability was restored to an exhausted country. The monarchy was strengthened and became hereditary again in a single royal house. Prosperity was gradually regained, and England received the stimulus of the Renaissance now moving north from France.

Although these events might not appear particularly auspicious for the growth and development of parliament, that institution actually made substantial gains under the Tudors, who, perhaps following the Lancastrian tradition, showed a remarkable deference to parliament—a deference frequently repaid by obsequiousness. The protestations of mutual respect that were exchanged by sovereign and parliament through most of the Tudor period contrast strongly with the centuries of conflict between these two institutions in the later Middle Ages. The rich, powerful, and autocratic Henry VIII expressed a partially hypocritical deference to parliament when he told the Pope in 1529: "The discussions in the English parliament are free and unrestricted; the crown has no power to limit their debates, or to control the votes of their members. They determine everything for themselves, as the interests of the commonwealth require." [8]

The truth is that parliament never thwarted the king, so his lip service to the independence of parliament cost him nothing, while there gradually built up for parliament a prestige that served it well under the Stuarts, when there again arose serious differences between crown and parliament. The prestige of parliament during Henry's reign was further enhanced by its vast legislative output, greater in bulk than that enacted in all previous reigns.[9]

The charge that Henry VIII's parliaments were subservient, however, may miss the point. The significant distinction between them and the important medieval parliaments lies in the fact that, by and large, Tudor parliaments were in agreement with the king. It is not, however, necessarily servile to agree. One of the most distinguished of British legal historians has this to say for parliament's role in the great events of Henry VIII's reign:

> In the end it was better that parliament should for a while register the acts of a despot than that it should sink into the contempt that seemed to be prepared for it. The part which the assembled Estates of the Realm have to play in the great acts of Henry VIII may in truth be a subservient and ignoble part; but the acts are great and they are all done 'by the authority of parliament.' By the authority of parliament the Bishop of Rome could be deprived of all jurisdiction, the monasteries could be dissolved, the king could be made (so far as the law of God would permit) supreme head of the English Church, the succes-

---

[8] Cited in Taswell-Langmead, *op. cit.*, p. 247.

[9] A. D. Lindsay, *The Modern Democratic State* (London: Oxford University Press, 1943), p. 71.

sion to the Crown could be settled first in this way, then in that, the force of statute might be given to the king's proclamations. There was nothing that could not be done by the authority of parliament. And apart from the constitutional and ecclesiastical changes which everyone has heard about, very many things of importance were done by statute. We owe to Henry VIII—much rather to him than to his parliament—not a few innovations in the law of property and the law of crime, and the parliaments of Elizabeth performed some considerable legal exploits. The statutes of the Tudor period are lengthy documents. In many a grandiose preamble we seem to hear the voice of Henry himself; but their length is not solely due to the pomp of imperial phrases. They condescend to details; they teem with exceptions and saving clauses. One cannot establish a new ecclesiastical polity by half a dozen lines. We see that the judges are by this time expected to attend very closely to the words that parliament utters, to weigh and obey every letter of the written law.[10]

Elizabeth I was probably as successful as her father in getting her way with parliament and she was also as wise as he in avoiding frontal attack. In 1601, for instance, the queen instructed the courts to stay proceedings testing the legality of her power to grant monopolies, the power that she is said to have called "the chiefest flower in my garden and the principal head pearl in my crown and diadem." Shortly thereafter, a lengthy debate on the issue commenced in parliament, where the sentiment was definitely hostile to the queen's position. Elizabeth immediately summoned the speaker of the House of Commons and capitulated "of her mere grace and favor" on the question of monopolies; at the same time, she threatened "with severe punishment according to their demerits" whosoever of her subjects should "presume to call in question the validity of her prerogative royal annexed to her imperial crown." [11] These are

[10] Frederic W. Maitland, "English Law, 1307–1600," originally published in *Social England*, reprinted as ch. V in Frederic W. Maitland and Francis C. Montague, *A Sketch of English Legal History* (New York and London: G. P. Putnam's Sons, 1915), p. 107. See also Pollard, "Parliament," in Pollard, *op. cit.*, pp. 104–129.

[11] Charles Howard McIlwain, *Constitutionalism Ancient and Modern* (Ithaca, N.Y.: Cornell University Press, 1940), ch. 5.

brave words, but the action was not that of an absolute ruler. It was, however, the traditional response of a wise English sovereign who could benefit by history and who correctly valued the power of the people as expressed in parliament. As Pollard has said, "If you reckon up the kings of England between the Norman Conquest and the sixteenth century, you will find that half of them were temporarily or permanently deprived of power by popular or baronial insurrections." [12]

Although in the 118 years of the Tudor dynasty the power of parliament was perhaps more real than apparent, there is no denying its gradual growth of prestige. From the beginning of the sixteenth century to its end, the House of Commons increased from 296 members to 462. The initiative in the enfranchisement was local, not central, and came from the increasing desire for representation from borough and county.[13] In this way, parliament was prepared under the Tudors for its new tasks under the Stuarts.

It is understandable that an institution habituated to a mistress as charming, as subtle, and as diplomatic as Elizabeth should chafe under such stubborn and uncongenial masters as James and Charles. The crisis that developed brought about the rewriting of English parliamentary history. The acts that in the Middle Ages had been intended to achieve immediate goals assumed the importance of principles and in time became the basis of English constitutionalism. From the grave of a feudal Magna Carta that had long since served its purpose there arose the mythical magna carta that was to become a symbol throughout the world for political and social reform. The medieval parliament, so many of whose acts had been tentative, unpremeditated, and improvised, was transformed in the popular mind into a mythical parliament, the prototype of modern liberal democratic legislative institutions.

The first major contributor to English seventeenth-century

---

[12] *Op. cit.,* p. 115.

[13] L. B. Namier, "The Elizabethan Parliament," a review of J. E. Neale's *The Elizabethan House of Commons,* reprinted in Namier, *Avenues of History* (London: Hamish Hamilton, Ltd., 1952), pp. 103–114 at p. 108.

political theory died in the latter part of the fifteenth century. He was Sir John Fortescue, a former chief justice and titular chancellor to Henry VI, who followed his Lancastrian lord into exile and from thence wrote his studies on the British constitution.[14] Exile affects different men in different ways. It made Machiavelli bitter; it seems to have made Fortescue merely homesick. From south of the Channel he saw the English constitution somewhat inaccurately and through rose-colored glasses—red roses, of course, for Sir John's was a Lancastrian constitution in which parliament held great power and prestige.

Fortescue's nostalgic studies, both partisan and lacking in originality, received little attention in his day. They were a godsend, however, to the seventeenth-century democratic jurists of England, who raised Fortescue to the position of the foremost authority on the medieval constitution and common law. From this extolling of the common law the British judges, its authoritative interpreters, were able to raise themselves in the political struggle in England to a place of prominence such as their European brethren never attained. Since in the main they picked the winning democratic side, the common law in England and indirectly in America gained a prestige the effects of which are still with us.

The chief contemporary spokesman for parliamentary supremacy was Sir Edward Coke, an eminent British jurist and statesman under Elizabeth I, James I, and Charles I. In 1610 he, along with three other judges, officially informed the privy council that the king could not create any new crimes by use of his prerogative powers (i.e., without the consent of parliament) and that his prerogative was limited by the law of the land.[15] Thus a new parliament, a figment of the intellects of the common law jurists and of the radical religious and political thinkers, was grafted onto the history of the real parliament.

Systemized control of the royal prerogative by parliament, however, was a development of the Restoration. In the words of Henry Jones Ford:

---

[14] Particularly *De laudibus legum angliae*.

[15] See Taswell-Langmead, *op. cit.*, pp. 384–385.

Up to the reign of Charles II the tenor of royal authority was essentially barbaric. The king's power . . . was circumscribed by customs which he could not afford to disregard, but these related principally to distributions of favors and interest, and the sources of his power thus secured, he could do as he pleased. His position in this respect was much like that of an American political boss, whose exploitation of his opportunities for his own profit is viewed complacently so long as he is munificent in his behavior and is tolerably successful in providing for his adherents. But in theory the king's authority was indefeasible. . . . The modern constitutional remedy of a change of administration was not available . . . what was to be done in case of intolerable neglect and mismanagement on the part of royal authority? The personal characteristics of Charles II were . . . influential in determining the lines on which a solution of the problem was sought . . . he could not be trusted to make due use of funds put under his control. . . . The only way to provide that funds meant for public services should not be squandered on the pleasures of the court, was to supervise disbursements. The great shock to traditional ideas caused by arrangements of this character is reflected by a number of entries in Pepys' Diary. . . . The definite institution of parliament as an organ of systematic control dates from the steps taken to curb the profligacy of the king.[16]

The Glorious Revolution of 1688 and the subsequent series of foreign sovereigns (William III and later, after Anne, George I and II) further entrenched the authority of parliament. An unlimited and uncontrolled prerogative, often abused by British kings, was not to be entrusted by the British nation to a foreign prince. Cabinet government, which became the instrument through which parliament could effectually exercise its new power, got its start under Charles II. Gradually, its original attachment to the king diminished, until after the Reform Bill of 1832 and the consequent loss of royal patronage the responsibility of the cabinet was directly to parliament.[17]

[16] Henry Jones Ford, *Representative Governments* (New York: Henry Holt, 1924), pp. 119–121.

[17] See John P. Mackintosh, *The British Cabinet* (London: Stevens & Sons, Ltd., 1962).

In the reign of Queen Anne, parliament took another historical step forward in making the crown responsible for expenditures by prohibiting any appropriation the crown did not recommend. It is still a rule of the British parliament that only the government may propose appropriations. The convention of impartial speakers was an eighteenth-century acquisition. The nineteenth witnessed the abolition of rotten boroughs, the gradual democratization of the suffrage, and the rise of political parties. During these three and a half centuries, however, the principle of parliamentary government remained essentially the same. The great common law jurists of the early Stuart period, led by Sir Edward Coke, forged the British constitution and gave parliament its preeminent place in it. They were the precursors, the prophets of the Glorious Revolution as Locke was its apologist. Before their time, parliament grew without a plan or a purpose beyond that dictated by the expediency of the moment. Since 1688, the role of parliament as they saw it has not been seriously questioned; alterations in its competence, composition, and procedures have been made in the hope of improving its efficiency rather than of changing its functions. The true mother of parliaments is not the model parliament of Edward I or any other medieval gathering, all of which might better be called the Neanderthal men of parliamentary prehistory. The first modern parliament was the brainchild of the common law jurists and was conceived in the seventeenth century.

The Riksdag [18]

Swedish parliamentary history in its broad outlines parallels that of Great Britain. In Sweden, as in all Germanic countries, the oldest society was one of the family or tribe, ruled by tribal

[18] For the research in this section I am deeply indebted to Professor Helge Kjekshus of the University of Dar es Salaam.

justice that evolved slowly over the centuries. The legal protection thus provided was called *fried,* which could not be fully
enjoyed without being a member of an *ätt* (tribe). Each *land*
(district) had been settled by a tribe, and local legal systems,
each with its particular law, thus grew up in relative isolation.
This law, primarily an outgrowth of custom, was based neither
on the command of an authority nor on the enactment of any
specifically created legislative body.[19]

There was equality before the law among the free men, who
supported the fried by their participation in the *ting* (assembly),
where public affairs were discussed and legal disputes adjudi-
cated. Each land had its *landsting.* In the smaller community units (*härad* or *hundrare*) there existed a *häradsting* or
hundraresting. The tings convened with considerable ceremony
at set times of the year. Their rulings were the judgments of the
free men, and the execution of these rulings was left to the interested parties. Through this judicial function of the ting, the
preservation and gradual development of the legal system took
place.

The custodian of the law was the *lagman* (law man), who
stored in his memory the oral tradition of the law. Recitations
of the traditional law by the lagman were annual events of the
ting: the lagman had an important role in the meetings of the
ting and early became an elected public official.[20] His position
was specifically regulated in the *landslag* (land law). The lagman
played a prominent part in deciding the lawsuits brought before the ting, and thus was influential in the formulation of
the common law. He also became a political leader, and as wealth
became increasingly important in early Swedish society, there
was a tendency to select the lagman from among the most powerful families.

Tacitus states that there were kings in Sweden as early as A.D.
100. The extension of royal power came through conquest or

---

[19] See Ebbe Hertzberg, *A General Survey of Events, Sources, Persons, and
Movements in Continental Legal History* (Boston: Little, Brown & Co., 1912),
and Nils Herlitz, *Grunddragen av det Svenska Statsskicktets Historie* (Stockholm: P. A. Nordstedt & Sönner, 1936).

[20] Hertzberg, *op. cit.,* pp. 135–136.

submission, but in the early period the king's power varied from district to district. Later, a greater and more uniform subjection to royal power was established. Following the political unification of Sweden, the monarchs made efforts to unify the legal system. The work of the early Plantagenets in creating the common law of England was carried out in Sweden in the latter half of the thirteenth century by kings Birger Jarl and Magnus Ladelås, who attempted to create a uniform law and to legislate for the whole kingdom. Starting at the beginning of the thirteenth century, the oral tradition of the law had gradually been put in writing, and laws thus became the subject of the earliest written records in Sweden.[21] It is largely from these laws that we can reconstruct the old Swedish society.

As in England, the king became the disburser of justice in competition with the traditional tings. The independence of the king's law from the tradition and formalism of the tings made it possible for him to adjudicate through equity. Soon the royal justice was recognized as superior to the justice of the tings; the next step was for the king to control the composition of the local courts and the appointment of the lagman. Thus the whole judicial system received a royal imprint.

Parallel with the king's duty to uphold the law and the legal system ran the duty to give the people fair and equitable laws. In performing this duty, the kings were empowered to lay down principles that were binding for the future independently of legal precedents; it was in this form that in the eleventh century legislation in the proper sense of the term first appeared in Sweden.[22] The king's competence in the field of legislation was never in fact disputed after the twelfth century; but throughout the Middle Ages the basic view was that although the king might formulate law, it would not come into effect unless assented to by those with whose rights the new legal principles interfered. There was a wide sphere of legal relations in which the king

[21] Lester B. Orfield, *The Growth of Scandinavian Law* (Philadelphia, Pa.: University of Pennsylvania Press, 1953), p. 235.

[22] Herlitz, *op. cit.*, p. 29.

was sovereign: in his own lands, over churches, monasteries, towns, merchants, and people in his immediate service. But where an already existing independent legal system (landslag) was found, where, as McIlwain would say, *gubernaculum* ran into *iurisdictio,* the requirement for popular consent to changes made by the king was a reality. Royal decrees or laws were often approved by the different tings. Although this became only a formality as soon as the king gained control over the appointment of the lagman, the formality did help to create a democratic tradition. More important was the fact that royal law confirmed or replaced the old land laws. This development cleared the way for Magnus Erikson's Almänna Landslag, a unified law for the entire kingdom, established in the fourteenth century.

The Swedish kings were handicapped in their struggle for power by the fact that the Swedish throne was not acquired through inheritance—as was normally the case in England and France—but was elective.

The body that elected the king was the *Riksmöte.* It was described in the landslag and is believed to be the origin of popular representation on a national scale in Sweden.[23] Composed of representatives of each *landskap* (county) of the federation, "The assembly recognized no distinction of nobility or of ecclesiastic status; it represented the undifferentiated agrarian society of old," made up of the yeomen—the members of the ätt who enjoyed the privileges of the fried. The Riksmöte was the major peculiarity of Swedish constitutional development during the Middle Ages.[24]

The king's power lay first and foremost in the duty of every man to participate according to his abilities in defending the realm and in supporting internal peace and justice; this duty was regarded as a service duty to the king. It took on different forms, such as work duty, host duty to the king and his retinue, and equestrian military service on the part of the nobles.

[23] Nils Herlitz, *Nordisk Offentlig Rätt* (Stockholm: P. A. Nordstedt & Sönner, 1958), Vol. I, p. 94.

[24] E. Lönnroth, "The Representative Assemblies in Medieval Sweden," International Convention of Historical Sciences, Rome, September 4–11, 1955, *Riassunti delle comunicazioni,* Vol VII, Florence, pp. 4–5.

Taxes were alien to the traditional law of Germanic tribes, where they were regarded as below the dignity of free men. By 1200, however, service duties had changed to tax obligations as money grew in importance. Monetary income was first obtained from territories like Uppsala and Öd, belonging to the crown, not to the king in person. This income was supplemented by fines, for an infraction of the law was considered a tort against the king's justice and an indemnity had to be paid to the king. Even murder was punished by fines, which were sometimes extremely high.[25]

Annual payments to the king in money or in kind became common practice around 1200. The landslag accepted this principle and also recognized that extraordinary taxes might be necessary from time to time, but stipulated that no new taxes could be levied without the consent of the different estates, clergy, nobility, burgesses, and peasants, through their representatives.

With the introduction of the landslag and the gradual extension of royal justice, there developed the practice of royal appointments of the *lagman* (later *länsman* or *fogde*) and the incorporation of the local land governments and courts as parts of the royal government. Thus the old ting changed from a political body to an administrative organ, and a public service—however amateurish and part-time by modern standards—was established. The growing stratification of society made it natural that the leading men in local affairs should become the link between the king and the people. Their service as representatives of the king, combined with the local basis of their prestige and interests, secured the continued working of a decentralized system. The men specially tied to the king's service were gradually distinguished as the *frälste,* the privileged class that later developed into the Swedish nobility. The traditional localism was still strong enough, however, for the king's men to become increasingly absorbed in and to act as part of the local foci of power, so that they ceased to consider themselves servants depending on the king.

[25] Herlitz, *Grunddragen*, p. 32.

In the later Middle Ages, a struggle for power was waged between the king and the *frälste* much as in England and France. The frälste wished to limit the king's claim to something like sovereign power in the name of a more democratic tradition. The nobility was powerful and the king could not rule without its support, but he also needed the cooperation and good will of the taxpaying peasants. The geographical realities of a vast, sparsely populated country, however, kept the federative conception of the kingdom alive, and the most important constitutional function of a medieval representative body—that of electing the king—was legally performed by the commons at a time when the arms and ideals of the nobility dominated Swedish policy as never before or later.[26]

The Swedes required the king to take an oath at his coronation that he would uphold the people's rights. This oath was prescribed in the landslag. The king swore (1) to protect the Church; (2) to support justice and truth and suppress injustice and falsehood; (3) to do no harm to rich or poor except according to law; (4) to choose Swedes and not foreigners for counselors and administrators; (5) to preserve the realm; (6) to live on the regular income of the crown property, and levy no new taxes except in an emergency and then in agreement with representatives of the people; (7) to uphold the law of the land and the privileges of the frälste, and to promulgate no foreign law without the consent of the people; and (8) to keep peace internally and defend the realm from foreign enemies.

The people answered the king through the lagman, agreeing (1) to respect the king's law; (2) to obey the king's commands when founded on law and decency; (3) to be his faithful servants in defending the kingdom; and (4) to pay in full all lawfully levied taxes. The ritual of these reciprocal promises constituted virtually a social contract.

After 1371, in addition to the traditional oath, the new king also issued a *Handfästing,* originally imposed by the frälste as a further restriction on the king's powers. The Handfästing con-

[26] Herlitz, *Nordisk Rått,* p. 4.

tained the specific promises and declarations of policy exacted by the nobility from the new king. The elective nature of the monarchy, when combined with the royal oath, the people's reciprocal oath of allegiance, and the Handfästing, made it appear that the monarch and the people entered into a legal compact. It was believed that a breach of this compact on the part of the king entitled the commons to remove him, such removal not being regarded as a revolution but as a legal procedure. Of the Swedish monarchs after Magnus Ladelås (1275–90) and before Gustav Vasa (1523–60), all but two were removed on these grounds.[27] Even after the monarchy became hereditary in 1544, it was believed that the people had retained the right to dispossess oath-breaking kings.

The Swedish kings of the Middle Ages did not succeed in eliminating local government autonomy for several reasons:

1. The king had no fixed income, and economic conditions forced him to move from place to place and to live off the crown possessions, thus preventing the establishment of a capital and permanently located central government organs.

2. Lack of continuity in the central government, and the rapid changes of kings, governors, and councilors, worked against the establishment of a fixed organizational pattern.

3. The powers traditionally exercised by local government severely limited the field left legitimately open to the central government.

The tradition of the ting gave Sweden the experience of popular assemblies. The ting, however, was a type of *Landsgemeinde,* a meeting of all the free men of an area rather than a representative assembly. By about 1200, the custom was established for the king to consult with the leading citizens of his realm. Thus a body, the *Herredag,* somewhat similar to the *curia regis,* was set up. The king summoned it at his discretion and determined its composition, which varied according to the matters to be discussed. As time went on, burgesses and peasants as well as nobles and clergy were summoned to the Herredag.

---

[27] Herlitz, *Grunddragen,* p. 23.

The Herredag was a large body and met intermittently. As in England, however, the king needed a small council of advisers and administrators in constant attendance; the name of this small permanent council was the *Riksråd*.

In principle, the king himself chose the members of his council, consisting of as many bishops and members of the clergy as he wished to nominate, and of no more than 12 of the secular nobility. The actual personal choice was limited, in that the most important men would have to be chosen, and the archbishop was a member *ex officio*.

In the fourteenth and fifteenth centuries, the Riksråd gained a firm reputation as a body of popular representation. The present dichotomy between central and local government had not yet developed: the men in the council were representatives of both *rex* and *regnum* in theory, but of *rex* and frälste in practice. After the king's court settled permanently in Stockholm, this representative character was gradually lost.

The Riksråd was particularly important under a weak king. It could not, however, provide the leadership or symbolize the state as effectively as a king. Therefore its power was often delegated to a single man called the *drot* or *marsk* (*c*.1430) and later (1470) the *riksförstandare* (governor). Several governors sought to enhance their personal position by going beyond the council for support. They therefore broadened the basis for their powers by appeals to the burgesses and the peasants, and so resulted a revival of the Herredag on a broader basis, called the *Riksdag*, which discarded the feudal system of representation and replaced it with the estates system.

Sweden's first Riksdag (parliament) in Arboga (1435) consisted of representatives of the peasants and burghers, along with the clergy and the frälste. The common people had played a part in the local governments at the time of the tings, but later were overshadowed by the rise in power of the frälste and the king. The change from the Herredag to the Riksdag marked a return of the other estates to a more active job in government.

As in England, however, the metamorphosis was a gradual one. The idea of the representation of the estates is found in documents dating from the middle of the fourteenth century.[28] In 1359, Magnus Erikson tried to get representatives of the peasants to a meeting of an assembly. Although the recognition of peasants and burgesses as members of estates was new, the resultant representation of the common people was less a post-feudal innovation than it was a return to an old Swedish custom formalized in the meetings of the Riksmöte.

The habit of convening popular assemblies in Sweden expressed itself in numerous other ways as well. *Landsortsmöten* (district meetings) were arranged when the king traveled in various parts of the realm in connection with county fairs or sessions of the local courts. Townspeople were summoned to *handelsdagar; kyrkomöten* (parish meetings) were held to discuss ecclesiastical matters.

The summoning of the Riksdag was originally an extraordinary event intended only for special occasions. The continual crises that occurred in Sweden in the last part of the sixteenth century explain how an institution designed originally to operate only in exceptional circumstances assumed an ever more normal place in Swedish constitutional procedure.[29] Sweden in fact became so dependent on the Riksdag that by 1660 triennial sessions were required by law.

The composition of the Riksdag depended entirely on the discretion of the royal councilors. It was convened to agree to major policy decisions that current belief held would need the approval of popular consensus. Such decisions included cases of treason, dethroning of the king, foreign policy, and new taxation. In all these instances, however, the Riksdag acted solely on the initiative of the government, and in the early period of its development its approval was not binding unless confirmed by the local councils. The Riksdag also evaluated complaints against the administration and thus performed a watchdog function over the administration in the public interest.

The political condition of Sweden when the Renaissance

[28] Lönnroth, *op. cit.*, pp. 4–5.
[29] Herlitz, *Grunddragen*, p. 84.

arrived was similar to that of England. Gustav Vasa (reigned 1523–60) was the Swedish equivalent of Henry VIII. Like Henry, Gustav came to the throne after the nobility had been seriously weakened (in England by the Wars of the Roses, in Sweden by the *Stockholms blodbad* [bloodbath] instigated in 1520 by Kristian II). Like Henry, by confiscating Church property Gustav achieved popularity and an economic freedom unparalleled in the preceding centuries. (The Roman Church and Kristian II had supported Erik of Pomerania's unpopular efforts to create a united Scandinavia.)

Gustav Vasa was elected king by the Riksdag in 1523. It was during his reign, in the parliament held at Västerås in 1527 that for the first time the Riksdag divided into estates for its meetings.[30] In 1544, Gustav brought about a constitutional change through parliament by which the monarchy became hereditary. This change was typical of the effects of the new learning that was influencing Sweden from the continent. The Swedes were taught that a *regnum* was a *patrimonium*, and that the authority of the sovereign over his subjects was absolute.

Gustav Vasa himself had too much real authority to worry overmuch about the theoretical justification of his power. This justification was strongly asserted by Johan III, the second of his sons to reign, and by his grandson Sigismund. They argued that the estates, in making the monarchy hereditary, had signed away their right to participate in the government and that the king had his authority from God, not from the people. The Lutheran Church accepted this theory. (The Roman Catholic Church, on the other hand, by its insistence on the separation of state and Church in Sweden had been able to reconcile the absolutism it claimed for its dogmas with a tolerance for the concepts of limited government and government by consent in the secular field. Martin Luther, the religious liberator, brought consent to the religious sphere and absolutism to the state.)

Again as in England, the modern liberal democracy in Sweden

---

[30] Hjärne Harald, *Reformationsriksdagen i Västerås* (Stockholm, 1893), p. 52, cited in Raymond Fusilier, *Les monarchies parlementaires* (Paris: Editions ouvrières, 1960), p. 62.

arose out of the popular antagonism to the forces of absolutism of the sixteenth and seventeenth centuries.

The absolutist ideas were not well received in Sweden, particularly since Gustav Vasa's heirs had far less personal stature than he and could not command respect for extra-constitutional deeds. Opposition to the Vasa kings arose among the nobles. Acting perhaps on purely selfish motives, they were able to argue that they sought to safeguard the constitutional system of the landslag, and to reestablish the governmental system on its basis.

The power of the nobles was demonstrated in their revolt against Erik XIV that resulted in his removal. When Johan III came to the throne in 1569 he was required to take an oath to respect the powers and privileges of the most important estates. On Johan's death, the throne fell to Sigismund, king of Poland, who sought to reintroduce Catholicism in Sweden. At his coronation he took an oath along the lines prescribed in the landslag, and was further required to give his word that Sweden should remain Lutheran.

Sigismund, however, continued his pro-Catholic policy and met with opposition. The success of the opposition was aided by the presence in Sweden of another Vasa, Duke Karl av Södermanland. Sigismund allied himself with the high nobility and Karl with the other estates. This brought to issue again the question whether or not the king, as in the Middle Ages, was bound by a contractual relation to the estates, and whether further the estates could bring the king to task when his responsibilities to them were not fulfilled. In 1600, those of the high nobility who had sided with Sigismund were beheaded (*Lindköpings blodbad*). As a result, although the principle of the hereditary monarchy was confirmed, the principle of absolutism was rejected and the role of the estates in public life firmly established. It was on their confidence that the future kings relied for the justification and at times for the actual basis of their power.

In 1611, royal assent was given to the proposition that parliament must approve all legislation and declarations of war. It was also from this date that the Riksdag meetings were held in Stockholm and not in the various provincial capitals.

In 1634, parliament was formally divided into four estates—nobles, clergy, burghers, and farmers—and the medieval custom of confirming parliamentary decisions through action of the local tings was abolished.[31] Later in the century there was a countertrend toward absolutism. In 1660, for instance, during the reign of Karl XI, the Riksdag, dominated by the lower estates (who feared the nobles more than the king), held that the king was responsible only to God for his actions and permitted a significant change in the name of the cabinet from *Riksråd* (Council of State) to *Kungligaråd* (Royal Council). It has been said that King Karl alone of his Swedish contemporaries upheld the tradition that the landslag was binding on king and subject alike.[32]

On the death of Karl XII in 1718, his sister Ulrica Leonora was elected queen. Two years later, she was permitted to abdicate in favor of her Hessian husband, who became Frederick I. As in England, the advent of the foreign kings greatly reduced the authority attached to that formerly exalted position. Power was vested in the people as represented in the Riksdag, and no bill could become law without the consent of three of the four houses. Each house had its own speaker. The speaker of the House of Nobles was called the *landtmarskalk,* and those of the other houses, the *talman.* The talman of the House of Priests was the archbishop *ex officio,* but the other three speakers were elected by their respective houses. A joint committee, the *hemliga utscott,* composed of 50 nobles, 25 priests, 25 burgesses, and, exceptionally, 25 farmers, was the locus of supreme power during Riksdag sessions. This committee prepared and presented all bills to the Riksdag, and created and deposed all cabinets. The landtmarskalk presided over the Riksdag when it met in plenary session, and over the hemliga utscott.

The Swedish equivalents of William III and the early Georges, however, did not bring with them a Walpole, and Sweden's experience with parliamentary democracy in the eighteenth

---

[31] Fusilier, *op. cit.,* pp. 63–64.
[32] Herlitz, *Grunddragen,* p. 100.

century was not a particularly happy one. The Riksdag became the arena in which two corrupt and uncompromising factions weakened the country by their squabbles and their ill-advised policies. One faction, known as the Hats, was dominated by militaristic nobles in the pay of Louis XV of France, and the other, known as the Caps (that is, nightcaps), by economy-minded commoners bribed by Russia. The experiment ended in 1772 when the young king Gustav III staged a *coup d'état* that divested the Riksdag of much of its power. Gustav was able to gain the support of the lower estates for his reform, but the opposition of the nobles led to his assassination in 1792. A succession of weak kings followed Gustav III until the ascension in 1818 of the French general Bernadotte (Karl XIV Johann), who had been adopted by the childless Karl XIII. Karl and his successors have led Sweden peacefully back along the road of constitutional government and parliamentary democracy. The modern bi-cameral Riksdag was established in 1866.

Thus, thanks to the Riksdag and its predecessors, Hertzberg is able to say of the Swedish people that "they never passed through an entire reign during which the right of the nation's representatives to take part in legislation has been abolished in form or in fact." [33]

The États Généraux and the Parlements of France

French parliamentary history differs from that of England and Sweden in that it is a history of failure.

France in the Middle Ages was the prototype of the feudal state. In England, the feudal system was established only after William's conquest in 1066, and William and the two Henrys

---

[33] *Op. cit.*, p. 561.

who followed were wise and clever enough politicians to prevent loss of effective power to the feudal nobility. Sweden escaped feudalism almost completely. The feudal system was not conducive to legislation, as feudal law was believed to have been given once and forever. Thus by the end of the twelfth century, custom was still the basis of the legal system in France. According to the twelfth-century jurist Beaumanoir, the right to issue statutes, that is, to legislate, belonged to the king. It was, however, a limited right and in time of peace effective only within his private domain. It consisted primarily of the power (a) to grant what the Roman lawyers called *privilegia*, which acted like *ante factum* pardons that exempted specific individuals from the rigors of the law, and (b) to issue ordinances concerning legal procedure. The king's legislative power was considerably broadened in time of war or national emergency in order to permit him to do what was necessary for the national welfare. Similar "emergency powers" were held by the barons within their lands. For the king's peacetime legislation to be binding, he first had to consult his council.[34]

The rediscovery of Roman law and its study in the law schools in Italy and France reintroduced in the West the concept of secular legislation and of law as a command of the sovereign. The steady increase in the lands held directly by the Capetian kings at the expense of the holdings of the great barons and the new system by which the Third Estate paid taxes directly to the kings contributed to the crown's material ascendancy. The kings could therefore gradually realize the claims to legislative power that were derived from Roman jurisprudence.

The kings of France started legislating at about the same time as the kings of England. According to Esmein,[35] the first statute (*établissement* or *stabilimentum*) was issued in 1155 by Louis VII in the form of a proclamation of a peace, a ten-year truce of God. In order to be effective, however, the principal feudal

---

[34] Jean Paul Hippolyte Emmanuel Adéhar Esmein, *Cours élémentaire d'histoire du droit français* (1896) (13th ed., Paris: Librairie Recueil Sirey, 1920), pp. 536–538.

[35] *Ibid.*, p. 535.

barons had to agree to this proclamation; the king lacked the physical or moral power (not to mention the legal power) to enforce his will upon them.

The French approximation to the British parliament was the États généraux. The first two Estates, the clergy and the nobility, formed the élite of the feudal system and it was proper feudal etiquette to call them occasionally for consultation as a *curia regis*, particularly in national emergencies. The Third Estate, that of the bourgeoisie, was not a recognized part of the feudal system. It was highly esteemed, however, by the king's tax collectors, and the king soon found it expedient to consult with representatives of this new source of revenue.

The États généraux and the English parliament got under way at about the same time and originally served much the same purposes. Philip the Fair, a contemporary of Edward I, called the first joint meeting of the French Estates in 1302, primarily to seek support of the entire nation in his struggle against Pope Boniface VIII. He called them again in 1308 for a similar purpose when he was persecuting the Templars. Both Edward I and Philip IV used the sessions of parliament not just to gain the support of public opinion, legitimizing their policies by obtaining popular assent, but above all to levy heavier taxes, particularly on the merchant class.

Although French writers before Montesquieu (notably Bodin, Fénelon, and Saint-Simon) wanted an institution like the British parliament for France, the États généraux began early to develop in quite a different way. The conditions under which these representative institutions operated explain some of these differences; for one thing, England and Sweden were united countries with reasonably stable boundaries. In spite of England's intermittent border wars against the Welsh and the Scots, and threats of invasion, the English, like the Swedes, maintained effective control over their territory. France, on the other hand, was a divided nation still feudal in structure, composed in part of almost independent fiefs such as Flanders, Brittany, and the English possessions. Anglo-French wars and internal French feuding took place on French soil from the Middle Ages until the end of the sixteenth century, and only sporadically did a

French king have effective control over the territory to which he laid claim.

France therefore did not share the English and Swedish potential for a natural, rational growth of the state and its institutions. The administrative skills of Henry II and Edward I which united England under a common law and a coherent administration might have been wasted on a French king of the period. The power of the kings of England and Sweden did not depend on feudalism. The kings of France lacked this independence, for their prestige and their claim to royal dominion were based on anachronistic feudal rights rather than on election as in Sweden or conquest as in England.

In firmly establishing a common law based on custom, the English and Swedish kings increased their prestige and their wealth. But in doing so, they also strengthened the principle of *iurisdictio* and gave parliament a powerful weapon against absolutism. In France, on the other hand, the revival of Roman law lent support to the proposition that legislative power lay in the will of the king.

The weakness of the États généraux *vis-à-vis* the royal power as compared with the strength of parliament and the Riksdag can be seen in several ways. The English kings bargained for extraordinary taxes in parliament. The rates for each "estate" were determined, and were the same throughout the land. As the nobles and the clergy were not taxed in France, these Estates took little interest in this important phase of parliamentary activity,[36] and for the taxes on the Third Estate the real bargaining took place at the local, not the national, level between the king's officers and the units of local government (called *bailliages* in the north and *sénéchaussées* in the south). At one time, the États généraux had first to give a general assent to the special tax; but before long they were inveigled into granting the king a series of perpetual taxes. By 1441, when the nobles demanded that all taxes be voted by the Estates for limited periods, Charles VII could reply, apparently with popular backing, that the

[36] Daniel Waley, *Later Medieval Europe* (London: Longmans, Green & Co., Ltd., 1964), p. 243.

Third Estate preferred to pay the taxes the king ordered, avoiding the additional expense of assembling representatives of the Estates.[37] Thus the États généraux were in the long run unable to use the financial weapon to restrain and control their kings. Without the power of the purse, the États généraux were in a poor position to get positive action on their advice or their grievances, particularly as the traditional attitude of the nobles had been to seek independence from the crown rather than trying (as in England) to gain control of the government and to make no attempt to cooperate with other classes, seeing no community of interest with them.[38]

The États généraux were further weakened by the practice of the *mandat impératif.* Deputies were considered agents of the electors, and authorized only to act in accordance with the electors' instructions. Although this is a logical method of operating a democratic institution, it is an impractical one, particularly when the representative body is weak and its powers ill defined, and communication is slow. Such conditions limit the maneuverability and effectiveness of parliament and consequently strengthen the king. Indeed, many contemporary constitutions specifically prohibit this practice of instructed deputies.

Perhaps the greatest impediment to the growth of effective representative institutions in France was the early separation of powers and personnel between the États généraux and the parlements. Like the États généraux the parlements were derived from the feudal *curia regis.* The États généraux took over the meager legislative and representative functions of the *curia,* while the parlements assumed its administrative and judicial functions. The English parliament, on the other hand, retained most of the functions of the English *curia,* notably its judicial one, while remaining functions of policy formation and administration passed to the king's privy council, an institution that parliament gradually succeeded in rendering subservient. This split up of the functions of the French *curia regis* between the États généraux and the parlements was a fundamentally different

---

[37] Esmein, *op. cit.,* pp. 569–570, p. 60.

[38] Waley, *op. cit.,* p. 69.

division from that which occurred in England and Sweden and had much to do with the failure of the French to establish a successfully functioning representative institution.

Originally there was only one body functioning as a parlement in France and it traveled about the country as part of the entourage of a peripatetic king. Later it became stationary in Paris just as the courts and parliament became stationary in London. It was at this time that it assumed the name of *"parlement."* Thereafter, the various provincial capitals acquired their own parlements, with provincial jurisdiction.

The members of the parlements were recruited from the first two Estates, the nobles and the clergy. The Third Estate was not represented. In their personnel, therefore, the parlements were similar to committees of the British House of Lords; this resemblance was increased when all peers automatically became members of the parlement of Paris, which then assumed the powers and competence of a court of peers.

Though the parlements were originally only advisers to the king, who under the principle of *justice retenue* was not bound by their advice, they gradually acquired considerable power. No statute of the États généraux and no treaty had legal effect until they registered it, and such registration was a discretionary act performed only after an examination of the merits. The kings asserted that the parlements had only a delaying veto—the right to advise the king against ordering registration. When an impasse was reached between a stubborn king and a recalcitrant parlement, the king held a *lit de justice*—a meeting of the parlement in the king's presence; the king's power in this case was absolute, *de iure.* Even then, however, the parlements often had the last word, particularly when it lay within their discretion to enforce the act as they chose.

In moments of crisis, the kings or the kingmakers sought the sanction of public approval from both the États généraux and the parlement of Paris. At such times both institutions were invested with extraordinary powers, which in the turbulent conditions of France's transition from a feudal to a national state they had occasion to use from time to time. When, for instance, there was no easily discernible heir apparent to the throne, or when part of the national territory was to be alienated, the États généraux were convened and consulted. The parlement of Paris and the États généraux frequently took opposite stands on major political questions. The parlement of Paris, for example, endorsed the passage of the French throne to Henry V of England by the Treaty of Troyes, which the États généraux opposed. When the États généraux supported the papal view denying the right of a heretic to the French throne, the parlement of Paris issued a statement to the effect that any decree proclaiming a foreign prince king of France (in place of the Protestant Henry of Navarre) would be null and void.[39] The parlement of Paris also refused to register the decrees of Louis XIII and Louis XIV setting up a body of co-regents for their minor heirs; in both instances, the parlement selected a single regent of its own choice and granted him full powers.

With the advent of stable government in France following the ascension of Henri IV, the États généraux had no further chance to use their extraordinary powers. In fact, they were not convened for 175 years, until 1789 on the eve of the Revolution, and then they were an anachronism. Although the États généraux had performed useful service in certain periods of crisis, they failed to protect the French people from their tyrants and they failed to make of themselves an efficient instrument of French democracy.

Since the Revolution, France has had five republics, two empires, two monarchies, and two interregna under reactionary militarists. The various parliaments that have been established in this period have gained little strength or prestige from the traditions of the États généraux; the powers and functions normally attributed to the legislative organs and to the regular courts have been encroached on by the Conseil d'état, in a sense the descendant of the parlement of Paris. The student of French government, particularly of French democracy, should not lose sight of the importance of the Conseil d'état, whose powers, functions, and methods of personnel recruitment have not funda-

---

[39] This action was not so revolutionary as it might seem. Étienne Pasquier (1529–1613) had written in 1576: "C'est l'autorité du Parlement qui a fait nos Roys," Pasquier, *Lettres* (Paris, 1619), cited in Mastellone, *op. cit.*, p. 23.

mentally changed since the days of Napoleon. It is this essentially autocratic and paternalistic organ, free from popular control, that has grown in prestige in France, while parliament and parliamentarians have continually lost face.

This is the story of the genesis of three parliaments. Two are success stories. The third, as one leading authority has said,[40] ended in a miscarriage.

Thus Great Britain with its parliament and Sweden with its Riksdag have developed institutions that have played a major role in maintaining the liberties of their people and of orderly government, and that are expressions of the genius of their respective cultures. The French, who have been ever ingenious in devising new governments, have shown little genius for government. They failed to develop the États généraux into a guarantor of civil liberty or an effective instrument of government, and so, in spite of their major contributions to the theory of liberal democracy, they have been unable to make such a system work over an extended period of time.

After this biographical sketch of parliamentary origins, we can examine the legal and conventional limitations that have been placed on the power of parliaments.

---

[40] Esmein, *op. cit.*, p. 575, ". . . l'institution des États généraux avait avorté."

3.

THE LIMITATIONS PLACED ON PARLIAMENTARY SOVEREIGNTY:

Lessons in Avoiding the Practice of One's Preaching

Democracy

The word "democracy," and its derivatives "democrat" and "democratic," have a complimentary connotation today over almost the entire world. Political leaders, from right-wing fascists to left-wing Communists, wish to be considered democrats. Only a handful of petty tyrants are still sufficiently anachronistic to scorn democracy.

Yet "democracy" was used by Greek philosophers to describe the worst of all governments. For them democracy meant the rule of the mob, the political condition in which the community (the *polis*) was at the mercy of the passions and whims of the ignorant and ignoble masses.

The modern democrats in the West, buttressed on the spiritual side by Christianity and on the material side by the Industrial Revolution, have claimed that the masses were capable of wisdom and nobility. In so doing they have perhaps been guilty of exaggerating both the present level of development and the potential for progress of the masses, who, as they would have it, are at once the source of political power and the object for whose benefit political power should be exercised. These democrats, however, have been considerably more sober in their practice than in their speech; and though they have kept the word "democracy" to describe the kind of political rule that they have attempted to establish, they have had in mind a government of law, not of men (and *a fortiori* not of the rabble). The content of this law, which the democrats of the West have placed over the rabble, is found in the philosophy of liberalism; the kind of government that results from the super-imposition of liberalism on democracy is called liberal democracy.

Liberalism

Liberalism is a philosophy of life with an ancient heritage. The core of this philosophy is found in Aristotle's *Ethics*; its other essential elements are eloquently presented in Milton. Yet its dominance as a political philosophy came only after the American and French revolutions.

Aristotle's major contributions to liberalism lie in three postulates: (1) that the purpose of individual existence is the growth of the individual in virtue; (2) that the purpose of social life is the establishment of social conditions that best favor this growth; and (3) that virtue lies only in acts both good in themselves and freely and willfully performed. Milton's contributions are the propositions that (1) no finite mind can grasp the absolute truth, so that everyone is subject to error, and that (2) the best way to improve one's understanding of truth is through the comparative method of examining conflicting opinions. Among the most significant later expositions of and speculations on political liberalism are those of John Stuart Mill (*On Liberty*, 1859) and Thomas Hill Green (*Lectures on Political Obligation*, delivered in 1879, published 1882).

Liberalism's contribution to democratic theory is thus teleological: it sets a purpose for social action against which its appropriateness may be determined. It is therefore a limitation on the power of *vox populi*, sanctioning it only when it wills *bonum publicum*—the common weal. Under liberalism, the expressed will of the people is not a legitimate source of law unless that will expresses a reasonable intent to further the goal of liberalism. God, according to St. Thomas, may not alter the eternal law because in so doing he would alter his own immutable nature. According to the liberal philosophy, when the people seek to betray their own nature by disregarding natural law, they are not speaking *ex cathedra* from their sovereign throne and their pronouncements are therefore not valid law.[1]

Constitutionalism

The procedure by which the philosophy of liberalism has been superimposed on democracy is called constitutionalism. Although this procedure may be used to establish regimes quite at variance with liberal democracy (by orthodox Moslems, for instance, who regard the Koran as the constitution), because of liberal democracy's reliance on constitutionalism, this term is often used as a synonym for liberal democracy itself. The same meaning is frequently ascribed to two other terms, "constitutional government" and "limited government."

It is helpful to begin an examination of the process of constitutionalism by distinguishing between two interrelated meanings of the term "constitution."

In its broadest sense the word "constitution" designates the fundamental structure and purpose of an institution. It is to this type of constitution that Sir Ernest Barker is referring when he says, "Constitutions are like poets, *nascuntur, non fiunt*." [2]

---

[1] For an account of the rise of liberalism in each of the major European countries, see Guido De Ruggero, *Storia del liberalismo europeo* (Bari: Laterza, 1925); English translation, *The History of European Liberalism* (London: Oxford University Press, 1927).

[2] *Political Thought in England* (London: Oxford University Press, 1915),

All social institutions have constitutions in this sense. In the field of public law, however, the word is frequently used to refer to a specific document in which the fundamental structure and purpose of an institution are purported to be found. This document is also referred to as the written constitution; and a state like the United Kingdom, which lacks such a document, is said to have an unwritten constitution, although the greater part of it is actually in writing.

Constitutions in the former sense are made up of laws and conventions. The laws are the juridically enforceable part. They will be found in the main in the written constitution, if one exists, but also in other fundamental laws that by chance are not contained in the written document.

The conventional part of a constitution is not enforceable at law; it is primarily unwritten. Conventions are slow-growing social usages, embodied in tradition. They are enforced by the diffuse sanctions of the society rather than by the legal, organized sanctions of the state. There is less discussion of the conventions than of the laws because the strength of the former lies in the consensus of opinion behind them, and by the time they become a subject of serious controversy they have already lost their conventional character. It is a convention, for instance, that the queen of Great Britain assents to petitions received in due form from parliament. Another convention restrains the British parliament from perpetuating itself in office or from legislating for the divers dominions beyond the seas.

Constitutions in the latter sense are made up primarily of laws, all of which, however, need not be constitutional in the former sense. Some provisions may be anachronisms, once important but no longer so, such as the provision in Amendment III of the American constitution regulating the quartering of troops. Or they may concern matters of too small moment to be of true constitutional importance, but ones over which the legislature could be expected to endure particularly heavy pressure by special interests. Examples of such provisions are the regulation

---

ch. VI, para. 4. See also Santi Romano, *L'ordinamento giuridico* (1918) (2d ed., Florence: Sansoni, 1945).

of the cutting of ski trails in the New York constitution and the numerous specific debt limitations for local government agencies found in several state constitutions. Such provisions are nonconstitutional in nature in that they do not concern the fundamental structure or purpose of a state; they are constitutional in effect in that they purport to be hierarchically superior to statute law.

The need for a constitution embodied in a written document is felt most strongly at the time of the formation of a new state or after a successful revolution. Such a document is not only a statement of principles and a description of an institutional framework; it is above all an ersatz tradition. The existence of a satisfactory tradition, as in Great Britain, New Zealand, and Sweden,[3] obviates the necessity of a constitution in this sense. The only recently established state to be formed without a "written" constitution is Israel. In this case an extraordinarily tenacious general will toward survival brought about a *de facto* unity of purpose, which overcame the disintegrating factor of basic disagreement—in good part religious—on the nature and contents of a written constitution.

Limitation of the legislative power of parliament is an essential feature of the constitution of a liberal democracy, whether that limitation be found in the legally valid written part of the constitution and among the constitutional conventions, as is the case of most modern states, or solely in the latter, as in Great Britain.

The degree to which legal provisions of a constitution limit majority will depends on the difficulty of the amending process. The most rigid constitutions are those, like the one with which Georgia was once saddled, that are not amendable. The most flexible, like those of France's Third and Fourth Republics and the Italian Statuto of 1848, can be altered by ordinary legislation, and thus offer no legal protection against parliament. The strongest protection, however, is offered by convention rather

---

[3] The Swedish and New Zealand constitutions are difficult to classify. See, for New Zealand, K. J. Scott, *The New Zealand Constitution* (Oxford: Clarendon Press, 1962), pp. 1–31, and for Sweden, Nils Andrén, *Modern Swedish Government* (Stockholm: Almqvist and Wiksell, 1961), pp. 9–15.

than by law, for conventions are the true sinews of societies. A knowledge and understanding of what is and is not done according to convention is considerably more significant than a knowledge of what can or cannot be done according to law. The bushman, or the freshman, who asks what would happen if the queen did not assent to a petition received in due form from parliament is asking a question that can be restated as: "What would the British constitution be if it were not what it is?"

Thus the British are content with and successful in operating a liberal democracy in which all the restrictions on parliament are merely conventional. Lord Birkenhead once courteously understated the British case to an American audience in the following words: "The decision is premature whether you and those who agree with you, have been right in trying to shackle the free will of the people by judicial control or whether we have been right in trusting the free will of a free people to work out their own salvation." [4] The strength of constitutional conventions in England being what it is, one wonders if the restraints on members of parliament in Great Britain are very different in effectiveness from those imposed on American congressmen and senators.

The liberal democratic philosophers who inspired the new constitutions were considerably less sanguine than Lord Birkenhead about the potential danger of parliamentary tyranny. In spite of the British example before their eyes, they were not content to rely merely on conventions to restrain the majority in the legislature.

A clearly reasoned defense of limited government is found in Vattel. The Swiss jurist's argument on this point is particularly interesting in that it is not based on natural law arguments. He holds that the legislature should not change the constitution, because the stability of the constitution is important for the welfare of the people, because the people have not empowered the legislature to alter the constitution, and because in changing

---

[4] Lord Birkenhead, *American Bar Association Journal,* IX (1923), 581.

the constitution the legislature would be altering the foundation of its authority.[5]

The limiting function of the constitution is of such paramount importance that it was thought proper to set down in Article 16 of the *Déclaration des droits de l'homme* that "a society in which there is no specific guarantee of civil liberties and in which the separation of powers is not established has no constitution." [6]

Fear of the masses was expressed with clarity and persistence by John Adams. The following expression of his thought on this is taken from a letter to Thomas Jefferson: "The fundamental principle of my political creed is, that despotism, or unlimited sovereignty, or absolute power, is the same in a majority of a popular assembly, an aristocratical council, an oligarchical junto, and a single emperor." [7] And Tocqueville is equally emphatic in his distrust of the majority. He argues that justice, not force, sets the limits of the law and that if it is wrong for a strong individual to mistreat a weaker one, it is also wrong for a majority to do an injustice to a minority.[8]

For the liberal democrat, then, *vox populi* is expressed in the constitution rather than in parliament, and the powers of parliament rather than stemming directly from the people are derived from the constitution.[9]

---

[5] Emer de Vattel, *Le droit des gens* (Neuchâtel, 1758), Book I, ch. III, para. 34.

[6] "... toute société, dans laquelle la garantie des droits n'est pas assurée, ni la séparation des pouvoirs déterminée, n'a point de constitution," cited in Romano, *op. cit.*, p. 3. See also Aristotle, *op. cit.*, Book IV, ch. IV, sec. 30: "When the laws are not sovereign, there is no constitution" (trans. Barker).

[7] Cited in Charles Edward Merriam, *History of American Political Theories* (New York: The Macmillan Company, 1903), p. 141. See also James Madison, *The Federalist*, No. X.

[8] "La justice forme la borne du droit de chaque peuple. ... Ou si vous admettez qu'un homme revêtu de la toute-puissance peut on abuser contre ses adversaires, pourquoi n'admettez-vous pas la même chose pour une majorité?" Tocqueville, *op. cit.*, Part II, ch. 7, sec. 3.

[9] "In a constitutional state persons are only obeyed in virtue of the authority given them by the constitution, and acceptance of the constitution is prior to obedience to persons. In constitutional states, therefore, the consti-

Unrepresentative Parliaments

The minority's fear of majority rule has at one time or another been expressed in all liberal democracies by maintaining or establishing undemocratic methods of parliamentary representation.

A method frequently employed in the past for limiting the democratic nature of parliamentary representation was to limit the suffrage. Property qualifications were at one time the rule. Today they are obsolete in parliamentary elections except in South Australia, Tasmania, and Northern Ireland, where they are still in effect for elections to the Legislative Council. Plural voting was once practiced in Sweden, Belgium, and Great Britain, but has now been abolished in these states. Rural overrepresentation, long an American practice, is slowly bowing out as a result of a Supreme Court decision.[10]

Since World War II, however, the suffrage has been extended to a point beyond which few would wish to go. The exception is Switzerland, where women can vote only in the three French Protestant cantons (Geneva, Neuchâtel, and Vaud), in one German Protestant canton (Zurich), in a half canton (Basel Stadt), and in the Italian canton (Ticino), but then only in local elections and those for the Conseil des états. In some places (for example, Italy) even illiterates may vote. The present tendency is to reduce the age requirements, and as of 1970 Norway and four states of the United States (Alaska, Georgia, Hawaii, and Kentucky) permitted persons under twenty-one to vote. (The popular argument in favor of this is that if a boy is old enough to be drafted he is old enough to vote; the argument is not rele-

---

tution is sovereign"—Lindsay, *op. cit.*, analytical Table of Contents 11 and 12 of ch. 9.

[10] *Baker* v. *Carr*, 369 U.S. 186 (1962).

vant to the question of what an eighteen-year-old girl is old enough to do.) The Netherlands, on the other hand, restricts voting to persons twenty-three years of age or older, and Italy requires voters in senatorial elections to be at least twenty-five. Various election laws virtually guarantee an unrepresentative parliament. The system of the single-member district and the possibility of victory by a plurality distorts the representative nature of parliament. The practice of rectifying systems of proportional representation so as to prevent parties that receive a small percentage of the total vote from having their just proportion of seats is a modern device that achieves the same general purpose.[11]

Australia, Canada, France, Great Britain, New Zealand, and the United States normally use the traditional system of the single-member district. Belgium, Denmark, Ireland, Italy, the Netherlands, Norway, Sweden, and Switzerland use various systems of proportional representation. In Germany, although approximately 50 per cent of the seats in the Bundesrat are filled by a single-member district election procedure, the overall composition of the chamber is determined according to the principles of proportional representation. Some of the systems of proportional representation use formulas for determining who has been elected that are as incomprehensible to the layman as the most abstruse thoughts of Einstein or the phenomenologists. In at least two cases, those of the Italian regions of Sicily and Trentino-Alto Adige, the legislators themselves knew not what they wrought and produced mathematical monstrosities.[12]

Upper houses were a virtually ubiquitous device to limit the voice of the people in parliament. Bi-cameralism arose out of the aristocratic organization of society, which tended to separate the major pressure groups along class lines. We have seen that the medieval parliaments of England were not formally bi-cameral; they were merely large assemblies in which, as is usually

---

[11] Douglas Rae, *The Political Consequences of Electoral Laws* (New Haven, Conn.: Yale University Press, 1967).

[12] John Clarke Adams, "Enigmatica elettorale," *Il mondo*, October 25, 1960, pp. 5–6.

the case, some people were more important than others. Those others were often too shy to speak out before their betters and consequently they formed the habit of taking counsel among themselves, particularly when the interests of the important people, the great barons, did not reflect their own. The estates of France and Sweden were the bases of a multi-cameralism in these states that remained in operation in the former until the end of the eighteenth, and in the latter until after the middle of the nineteenth century.

The aristocratic quality of upper houses favored them for the role of moderators of democratic impulses. As despotisms gave way to democracy, the conservative element, although willing to entrust a popularly elected assembly with a share in the legislative power, feared the exuberance of vulgar and untried solons and took refuge behind a senate representing the wealthy and the well-born and holding a veto on legislative enactment.

When bi-cameralism is used to subvert the representative nature of parliament as *vox populi,* a method of determining membership of the upper house is devised or retained that will virtually assure a preponderant position to the establishment.

The British House of Lords is still primarily a hereditary body and all new appointees are nominated by the prime minister. Indirect elections for all members of the upper house are the rule for the Förste Kammar (Sweden), the Erste Kamer (Netherlands), and the Sénat (France), and for some members of the Belgian Sénat and the Swiss Conseil des états. Members of the Canadian Senate are appointed on nomination of the prime minister, and members of the Bundesrat are appointed by the Länder executives.

In federal states it is normal for the lower house to represent the people and the upper house the federated units, equally (Australia and the United States) or nearly so (Switzerland and Germany). In Canada, the senators represent a province only nominally. Members of the second chamber may be elected by universal suffrage (Australia, the United States, and most Swiss cantons), by the legislatures or executives of the federated units (Germany and some Swiss cantons), or appointed for life by the crown (Canada). From the founding of the United States of

America to the establishment of the United Nations, bi-cameralism in a federation, however, has actually been the result of a political compromise between power politics and democratic egalitarianism rather than of logical reasoning.[13]

No modern state employs a multi-cameral system as a regular procedure, although the Swedish constitution still requires the consent of the Lutheran clergy to changes in the Church laws and the privileges of the clergy (*Regieringsformen,* Arts. 87, 114). This vestige of tri-cameralism derives from the powers once held by the clergy in the traditional quadri-cameral parliament of Sweden, abolished in 1866. Yugoslavia adopted a five-chamber parliament in 1962.

Other methods of limiting the representative nature of parliaments include the extension of the term of office to eight years for the Förste Kammar, nine for the French Sénat, twelve for the Legislative Council of New South Wales, or to life (for the House of Lords and the Canadian Senate), and a high minimum age qualification for membership in the upper house. The proponents of functional representation have sometimes a bi-cameral system in mind with one house based on territorial and the other on functional representation.[14]

---

[13] See Walter Bagehot, *The English Constitution* (1867), ch. 4, para. 11. "It is said that there must be in a Federal Government some institution, some authority, some body possessing a veto in which the separate States Composing the Confederation are all equal. I confess this doctrine has to me no self-evidence, and it is assumed, but not proved. The State of Delaware is *not* equal in power or influence to the State of New York, and you can not make it so by giving it an equal vote in an Upper Chamber. The history of such an institution is indeed most natural. A little State will like . . . to see some token . . . of its old independence preserved in that Constitution by which that independence is extinguished. But it is one thing for an institution to be natural, and another for it to be expedient."

[14] For a detailed description of a system for functional representation, see Charles Benoist, *La crise de l'état moderne* (Paris: Didot, 1897), particularly ch. 6. See also Gaetano Mosca, *Le costituzioni moderne* (Palermo: Amenta, 1887), Ch. 4, sec. 3; Gabriele D'Annunzio di Montenevoso, "Carta della Reggenza del Carnaro," in *Por la più grande Italia* (Milan: Istituto nazionale per le edizioni di tutte le opere di Gabriele D'Annunzio, 1932); and Pierre Mendès-France, *La république moderne* (Paris: Gallimard, 1962), pp. 91–108.

Limitations on the Legislative Powers of Parliaments

Constitution makers have not been content merely to limit the representative nature of parliaments; they have been concerned to limit their legislative power as well. The *Déclaration des droits de l'homme* in the French constitution of 1789, itself copied after the British practice, established a precedent in constitution writing that has been copied more or less assiduously and effectively ever since. The American edition, which was omitted from the original constitution, was soon added by popular demand as the first ten amendments. The newer constitutions are likely to guarantee additional rights, such as the right to work and to education.

Constitutions may contain legislative prohibitions other than those found in a bill of rights. Some prohibit amendments that alter either specific articles of the constitution or its general principles and spirit. Thus the Italian constitution cannot be altered so as to reestablish the monarchy, the American constitution guarantees the equal representation of the federated states in the Senate, and the Norwegian constitution prohibits amendments contrary to its spirit.

Another method of limiting the legislative power of parliament is by enumerating in the constitution the subject matter over which parliament is entitled to legislate. This system is common in federations, where the powers of the national legislature or of the legislatures of the federated units are commonly enumerated. Thus the United States, Australia, Germany, and Switzerland operate under constitutions that enumerate the legislative powers of the federal legislature, while Italy operates under one that enumerates the powers of the provinces and regions. The Canadian situation is somewhat obscure on this point.

In the case of the federal states, it can be argued that a grant of enumerated legislative powers to one level of legislature and the relegation of the residual legislative powers to another level is really no limitation of parliament *qua* institution. The enumeration of legislative powers in a unitary state, however, is clearly so, as can be seen in France under the Fifth Republic. By the use of this expedient, de Gaulle and Debré so emasculated the French parliament that it is doubtful if France today deserves to be called a liberal democracy. The French constitution divides the subject matter over which parliament may legislate into two categories: civil rights, nationality, crimes, punishments, the judiciary, taxes, and nationalization are the principal matters over which parliament has normal legislative powers. Over national defense, local government, education, property rights, commercial law, labor law, and a few other matters it is empowered to enact skeletal legislation. Otherwise, legislative power is exercised by executive decree.

A common method of limiting the power of parliament to legislate is to require a favorable vote greater than a majority of a quorum. Thus it is not unusual to require an absolute majority (i.e., over 50 per cent of those entitled to vote) rather than a simple majority (i.e., over 50 per cent of those actually voting) to legitimize a legislative enactment. On other occasions, as for instance for the approval of constitutional amendments and to override executive vetoes, a $3/5$ or $2/3$ majority, either simple or absolute, may be mandatory. The purpose and effect of the filibuster is to require something close to a unanimous vote in parliament. And the *reductio ad absurdum,* the requirement of a unanimous vote, actually hamstrung the Polish parliament.

An American device for curtailing parliament is to place a constitutional limitation on the frequency and length of sessions. Thirty-one of the United States have biennial sessions, 23 states limit the number of days the legislature may sit, and 10, the number for which its members may be paid—an ingenious and insidious way of achieving substantially the same purpose. It has been said that no single fact has a greater effect on the legislative environment than constitutional restraint on the length of session.[15]

---

[15] Malcolm E. Jewell and Samuel C. Patterson, *The Legislative Process in the United States* (New York: Random House, Inc., 1966), p. 138.

Exercise of Legislative Power by Other Than Legislative Organs

In spite of the lip service still paid to the doctrine of the separation of powers, modern constitutions actually give considerable legislative power to nominally executive and judicial organs.

Executive organs are frequently involved *de iure* with the preparation of legislation. In parliamentary systems, where the government is a creature of the legislature, the opinion of some other executive organ is frequently required before submission to parliament of a government bill (or in some cases of any bill). The Conseil d'état, or some similar administrative body, performs a consultative function in France, Holland, Italy, and Luxembourg. In Italy, there is the further requirement that the president of the Republic approve all government bills before their submission to parliament (Constitution, Art. 87).

In several states, convention has virtually deprived parliament of legislative initiative. Thus in Switzerland the *de facto* situation is that all bills originate in the Federal Council, while in many other states (e.g., Great Britain, Germany, the Netherlands, France, Sweden, Canada) the right of a member of parliament to initiate legislation on his own is severely limited.

The power to issue decrees with the effect of law during emergencies is a universal and inalienable component of the executive power. The British refer to this and other "exclusive privileges of the crown" as the royal prerogative. Emergency power is more often derived from convention and common sense than from constitutional law. The constitution of the Fifth French Republic (Art. 16) spells out the emergency powers granted the French president. They give absolute power to the president on a contingency basis and further grant him exclusive power to proclaim the existence of the conditions upon which the exercise of emergency power is contingent. In those states—and they are the majority—where the emergency powers exist only by convention there would appear to be a greater check on the executive, as it would seem necessary to have something close to consensus on the existence of the emergency before the executive's emergency powers would be operative.

An executive veto is a normal part of a presidential system of government. It is found in the American federal government and in 49 of the 50 states. The Swiss Federal Council has a conventional rather than a juridical veto power, since, as we have seen, it is the Swiss tradition that all bills emanate from the Council.

In parliamentary systems it is difficult to speak of the government's veto power, as no government is possible without the cooperation of the parliament and the cabinet. Thus the head of the government can veto any private member bill so long as he holds the confidence of the majority of parliament. In some parliamentary systems, the head of the state has a veto power. The president of Italy has used this power sparingly,[16] while the king of Norway has virtually lost it through disuse.[17] Perhaps the last king of England who believed he had the veto power was George III, who wanted to use it to prevent the enfranchisement of Roman Catholics; but in theory a law enacted by parliament is still merely a petition until the monarch assents.

The Conseil constitutionnel of France exercises a veto power over legislation. Whether this Conseil is *de iure* an executive or a judicial body is perhaps debatable; the weightier arguments suggest the former.[18] *De facto* it is unquestionably a tool of the executive.

Liberal democratic constitutions often give the executive the power to dissolve one or both houses of parliament. If the power extends to both houses, the executive may normally dissolve

---

[16] See John Clarke Adams and Paolo Barile, *The Government of Republican Italy* (2d ed., Boston: Houghton Mifflin Company, 1966), pp. 79–80.

[17] See James Storing, *Norwegian Democracy* (Boston: Houghton Mifflin Company, 1963), pp. 54–55, 91.

[18] See Mauro Cappelletti and John Clarke Adams, "Judicial Review of Legislation: European Antecedents and Adaptations," *Harvard Law Review,* LXXIX (1966), 1207–1224.

the houses singly or concurrently. In Great Britain, France, and Germany, however, only the lower house may be dissolved, and in Norway, Switzerland, and the United States no power of dissolution lies with the executive.

The power to dissolve parliament was once part of the royal prerogative, an expression of the legal ascendancy of the king over an assembly of his subjects.[19] It was thus a traditional check on representative government. Only in France among the major western powers today does the power of dissolution remain unequivocally in the hands of the chief of state, and only there does it serve to strengthen the hand of a nonparliamentary executive power *vis-à-vis* the parliament.[20] In order to prevent such an undemocratic use of this power, other states require the countersignature of a responsible minister or ministry to validate a dissolution decree. Only in France is there no such legal or conventional safeguard.

In nineteenth-century liberal democratic theory and practice, dissolution was intended to help establish an equilibrium between the separated legislative and executive powers, and to overcome deadlocks between the organs exercising these powers. Thus, dissolution was resorted to when the executive and the legislature failed to cooperate. Under this theory, dissolution, rather than being a weapon against representative democracy, was a weapon against a presumably unrepresentative parliament. It appears that only in the Netherlands, where the ties that link parliament and government are unusually tenuous, does this function retain primary importance today.[21]

In Germany, it would appear that the purpose for giving the president a limited power of dissolution was actually to strengthen the Bundestag against the executive.[22] According to the German constitution, so long as the Bundestag can agree on

[19] See Jacques Velu, *La dissolution du parlement* (Brussels: Établissements Émile Bruylant, 1966), pp. 236–239.

[20] *Ibid.*, pp. 477–507.

[21] *Ibid.*, p. 398.

[22] Georges Burdeau, *Traité de science politique* (7 vols., Paris: Librairie de droit et de jurisprudence, 1949–57), Vol. VII, pp. 345–346.

a new chancellor by an absolute majority vote, the president and the outgoing chancellor are powerless to dissolve it. In practice, however, the German system of so-called constructive vote of no confidence has appeared to fortify the chancellor rather than the Bundestag. Moreover, the dogma of conventional wisdom to the effect that the threat of dissolution on the part of the executive gives the executive the whip hand over the legislature and leads to greater government stability is not borne out by a comparison of stability in states that (1) use dissolution or the threat thereof frequently, (2) use them rarely, and (3) have no powers of dissolution.[23]

Many liberal democratic constitutions enable the courts to limit the power of parliament. The major method employed is the judicial review of legislation.

The justification of judicial review of legislation is simple and reasonable. It goes like this: the judicial power determines the validity of inferior norms and declares them *ultra* or *inter vires* depending on whether they are within the authority of the issuing body to enact. A rigid written constitution creates a series of legally binding norms with which all legislation must be compatible. The determination of this compatibility (i.e., the decision as to whether in a given situation parliament has acted *inter* or *ultra vires*) is just as much a judicial question as the determination of the compatibility of a regulation with the law alleged to have authorized it. It therefore falls into the normal judicial power.

The first state to make extensive use of judicial review was the United States, where the extension of this practice was favored by a series of circumstances, including the legalistic nature of America's justification for seeking independence (e.g., the Declaration of Independence), which gave great prestige to law and the courts, and the prevalence of the theory of checks and balances, which condoned the checking of one institution by another. The federal nature of the United States, and the doctrine of the limited powers of the federal government, made

[23] Velu, *op. cit.*, pp. 290–292.

it virtually necessary to empower some institution to resolve the numerous and inevitable disputes that would arise over the boundaries of competence of the competing organs.

More important perhaps to the success of judicial review in the United States was the application to the American legal system of the common law principle of *stare decisis*, which makes a decision of a high court a binding precedent on lower courts. Once the principle of *stare decisis* is accepted, the question whether the court invalidates the law or merely refuses to apply it in the case at hand becomes purely academic, as once the Supreme Court has spoken, all other courts must follow.

The other significant feature of the American system of judicial review is the practice of determining constitutional questions only as they arise incidentally to the adjudication of another dispute. Anglo-American judges shy away from declaring the law from arguments based on broad and general principles. It is a common law principle, in fact, that any reasoning in a judicial decision not necessary to the settlement of the dispute is an *obiter dictum*, not a binding precedent. Judges brought up in this tradition have had little difficulty in coming to the conclusion that a legal issue that does not arise from a specific dispute is nonjusticeable. Only when required to do so by the constitution (e.g., Colorado, Florida, Maine, Massachusetts, New Hampshire, Rhode Island, and South Carolina), by statute (e.g., Alabama and Delaware, the Dominion of Canada and its ten provinces[24]), and by convention (e.g., North Carolina) do courts in the common law tradition consent to give advisory opinions on constitutionality.

Judicial review is used as a constitutional restraint on legislative activity in several European countries. The power is exercised by the regular courts in Norway and Denmark and by special courts in Austria, Italy, and Germany. The regular federal court of Switzerland exercises this power over the constitutionality of cantonal statutes, with respect both to the federal and the relevant cantonal constitutions. Judicial review is not found

[24] See J. A. C. Grant, "Judicial Review in Canada: Procedural Aspects," *Canadian Bar Review*, XLII (1964), 195–224.

in Great Britain, Belgium, France, or the Netherlands, but the regular courts of Ireland and Sweden appear to be assuming the power of judicial review of legislation.[25] Judicial review in Norway would appear to extend to constitutional amendments, as Article 112 of the Norwegian constitution states in part that "amendments must . . . never contradict the principles embodied in this constitution, but merely relate to modification of particular provisions that do not subvert the spirit of the constitution."

Unlike the other countries that employ judicial review to protect the constitution from legislative inroads, Austria, Italy, and Germany have bypassed the regular courts and established special courts for this purpose. They have been led to do this in part out of deference to the French concept of as complete as possible a separation of powers, and in part because *stare decisis* is not a principle of these judicial systems. Granting the regular courts the power to overrule the legislature would thus for them constitute a revolutionary step in the constitutional tradition. Without the convention of *stare decisis,* the decision would only affect the case at hand and a court would be free to apply a law that a superior court had previously considered unconstitutional.

The actual power of the Austrian, Italian, and German courts is considerably enhanced by the fact that the judges come only in part from the regular judicial hierarchy. In these countries, the position of judge is part of a civil service career. One enters as a young man and if one succeeds in favorably impressing the higher ups in the administration, it is possible to climb to the top. Like other career civil servants, the successful judges learn to operate within the law and are discouraged from questioning its validity. The mentality thus developed is not conducive to juristic iconoclasm. Whereas judicial review of legislation in theory is merely a logical extension of the function of adjudication, in practice it is radically different. Adjudication—the work of ordinary courts and ordinary judges—falls well within

[25] See J. M. Kelly, *Fundamental Rights in the Irish Law and Constitution* (2d ed., Dublin: Allen Figgis, 1967), and Mauro Cappelletti, *Il controllo giudiziario di costituzionalità delle leggi nel diritto comparato* (Milan: Giuffrè, 1968), pp. 55-56.

the confines of administration; judicial review of legislation, however unwilling some judges are to admit it, is essentially determination of policy. As such, its exercise is often incompatible with the mentality normally developed by the career civil servant.

The Austrian, Italian, and German courts (called, respectively, the *Verfassungsgerichtshof,* the *Corte costituzionale,* and the *Bundesverfassungsgericht)* are all required by law to give advisory opinions in disputes over competence between the legislature and other organs of the state. The Verfassungsgerichtshof will also determine the constitutionality of a law at the request of either of Austria's supreme courts (the *Oberster Gerichtshof* and the *Verwaltungsgerichtshof*—the latter hears administrative cases). The Corte costituzionale will do this at the request of any court and all judges are required to refer to it all questions of the constitutionality of laws that are not patently groundless (*manifestamente infondate*) and/or pertinent to the decision of the case at hand, whether raised by the parties or by the judges themselves. The Bundesverfassungsgericht has the jurisdiction of the Corte costituzionale and, in addition, the obligation to hear the claim of any citizen who has been denied a constitutional right by federal or Länder legislation.[26]

Direct Democracy

The devices considered up to this point have had the purpose of containing parliament—on the theory that there is something inherently dangerous in popular sovereignty. Their supporters have been afraid of the tyranny of the majority and have wanted to temper the exuberance, the impatience, and the ignorance of the masses by leaving in aristocratic hands some controls, even if only of a delaying nature. The devices that now concern us

[26] Cappelletti and Adams, *op. cit.*

are of a different nature. They too are motivated by a distrust of parliament, but in this case the fear is Rousseau's fear that a representative parliament will nonetheless not represent the general will.

The ideal of those who support these devices is the direct democracy of the New England town meeting, of the Swiss Landsgemeinde, and of the school district meeting throughout much of the United States. In these cases, the community of citizens does its own legislating.

The undemocratic aspects of these systems are patent to those who have had experience with them. Even where the limited size of the group and its competence in dealing with the matters under discussion might make direct democracy appear feasible, there must still be, except in the case of very small bodies, a large gap between the theoretical right to speak and the actual ability to be heard. It is the chairman of the meeting who determines who is to speak, when he is to speak, and for how long. Jouvenel has observed, "There is no space (as far as I know) in the political theory of democracy for the simple and glaring fact of bottlenecks. Individuals are told at every moment that they have an equal right of free speech and they find out in any concrete instance that the opportunity of expression is denied them." [27]

Direct democracy persists, where it is still in operation, because of the inertia of tradition and because of democracy's undeniable emotional appeal and symbolic value. The thought that the community of citizens assembles to legislate for the general welfare is mildly soul-stirring, and to be against it is something like opposing mothers, babies, and dogs. But except for their ritual value, it is hard to find valid arguments for convening such assemblies. The famed New England town meeting is hard to defend today, and unless a certain John Trumbull was as bad a political observer as he was a poet, the following "verses" would seem to cast doubt even on the former efficacy of that institution:

[27] Édouard Bertrand de Jouvenel, "The Chairman's Problem," *American Political Science Review,* LV (1961), 368–372.

As that fam'd weaver, wife t'Ulysses,
By night each day's-work pick'd in pieces,
And tho' she stoutly did bestir her,
Its finishing was ne'er the nearer;
So did this town with stedfast zeal
Weave cob-webs for the public weal,
Which when compleated, or before,
A second vote in pieces tore.
They met, made speeches full long winded,
Resolv'd, protested, and rescinded;[28]

It is difficult to speak with authority on the Landsgemeinde, as this institution remains a minor mystery of liberal democratic government. When a Landsgemeinde meets and all the males of a Swiss canton convene, there is little room for foreign observers. The practice is to invite a half-dozen dignitaries from other parts of Switzerland to attend and to hope no one else shows up. The exclusiveness of the Landsgemeinde can be justified by the physical limitations of the hamlets where it is held, but it is probably motivated as much or more by the ritualistic nature of the event. It is a private festival of a closed group where the stranger is *de trop*.[29] Since the hopelessness of a Landsgemeinde for a community much larger than his native eighteenth-century Geneva was seen even by Rousseau, there has been no attempt to extend this system to more populous areas.[30]

[28] *M'Fingal, a Modern Epic Poem* (Hartford, 1782), reproduced in Albert Bushnell Hart, *American History Told by Contemporaries* (4 vols., New York: The Macmillan Company, 1901), Vol. III, pp. 80–81.

[29] See W. A. Liebeskind, "Gli arenghi della Svizzera," *Il ponte*, IV (1948), 763–766.

[30] An ingenious form of direct democracy was proposed by Moritz Rittinghausen in 1870 (Moritz Rittinghausen, "Uber die organisation der direkten Gesetzgebung durch das Volk," *Sozial Demokrat*. Pamphlet no. 4, Cologne, 1870). He proposed dividing up the nation into groups of 1,000 persons. The need for legislation on a particular subject would be suggested to the government by initiative. The government would then convene all of the assemblies, each in its own meeting place, to discuss the matter and draft the legislation, which would be passed or rejected by majority vote over the nation. If passed, a bill drafting committee of the government would coordinate the various bills submitted by the various groups of 1,000 citizens.

By the device of initiative and referendum, however, advocates for direct democracy were persuaded they had found the corrective for any undemocratic aspects of parliamentary behavior. Initiative and referendum have thus become important elements in Swiss political life. They are an effective means of legislation in many of the non-Landsgemeinde cantons, and probably the only reason they are not permitted for federal legislation is the fear of the tyranny of the majority on the part of the small Catholic cantons, protected by their equal representation in the Conseil des états. The Landsgemeinde tradition in Switzerland is a factor in the favorable reaction of the Swiss to initiative and referendum. Their satisfaction with the system led American radicals to endorse it in the early part of the twentieth century. Thus, although the system has never been adopted at the federal level, the radical Republicans of the Northwest gave it their full support and it became part of many of the state systems in that area and of a few elsewhere. Enthusiasm for the device of initiative and referendum, however, has of late been on the wane in the United States.

Initiative and referendum are provided for in the Italian constitution but as yet have not been implemented by enabling legislation, as parliament appears to be loath to so restrict its own powers. In some liberal democracies, referenda are used for proposed constitutional amendments. This is the practice in the United States, Switzerland, France, and an inoperative provision of the constitution in Italy. In Switzerland, the amendment may be proposed by initiative. In the other countries, it must be first approved by parliament. In France, de Gaulle illegally bypassed parliament by amending the constitution through a plebiscite, which in this case is another name for a referendum. The Swedish, Danish, and Dutch practice of dissolving parliament after it has passed a proposed constitutional amendment, and re-

---

For a further exposition of this example of the Teutonic mind, see Roberto Michels, *Zur Soziologie der Parteiwesens in der modernen Demokratie: Untersuchungen über die oligargischen Tendenzen des Gruppenlebens* (Leipzig, 1910) (English trans. Eden and Cedar Paul [New York: The Free Press of Glencoe, 1949]), Part I, A, ch. 3, "Mechanical and Technical Impossibility of Direct Government by the Masses."

quiring another affirmative vote in the newly elected parliament, is similar in effect to a referendum.

Sweden and Australia have used a nonbinding referendum on issues of public interest on which the parties do not wish to take a stand. An example is the suggestion that traffic should drive on the right instead of on the left, as was the Swedish tradition. The Swedish parliament voluntarily consulted the electorate on this issue but did not feel bound by the result. Unless it becomes a convention that parliament must consult and be bound by the result, this practice merely gives an indication of public opinion (like a Gallup poll or an analysis of senatorial mail in the United States) and can be considered an aid to rather than a restriction on parliament. The British, who have no referendum, use the private member bill for much the same purpose: when these bills come to a vote, the members are normally uninstructed by their parties and as well as looking into their own consciences before voting, they are expected to seek to fathom those of their constituents.

Some German-Swiss cantons have a type of legislative recall called the *Abberufungsrecht,* according to which a given number of voters may institute a general vote by initiative as to whether a legislative (or executive) body should be divested of its power before the expiration of its normal term of office.[31]

Another device for controlling parliament, of purely historical interest, was the establishment of elective bodies whose function it was to see that the constitution was in operation. In the eighteenth century the states of Pennsylvania and Vermont set up such bodies, called in these cases Boards of Censors. They could "pass public censures . . . order impeachments . . . and recommend to the legislature the repeal of such laws as appear to them to have been enacted contrary to the principles of the constitution." [32]

---

[31] See Federico Mohrhoff, *La dissolution des assemblées législatives dans les constitutions modernes* (Rome: C. Colombo, 1953).

[32] The wording is from the Pennsylvania constitution of 1776, Article 47. A similar statement is found in Article 44 of the Vermont constitution of 1777, cited in Mario Battaglini, *Contributo alla storia del controllo di costituzionalità delle leggi* (Milan: Giuffrè, 1957), pp. 167–171.

The practice of holding constitutional conventions, or of calling a referendum at regular intervals on the question of holding a constitutional convention, is another method of giving the voters the power to act without having to rely on the legislature. The former system was advocated by Thomas Jefferson; the latter is in operation in several states of the United States.

Parliament thus has rarely had *carte blanche* to legislate as it saw fit. The exceptions are the notorious French conventions of 1792 and various constituent assemblies that assumed legislative powers while drafting a constitution (e.g., the Italian Assemblea costituente of 1946–48 and the Israeli Knesset of 1949). *Vox populi* may theoretically be the source of law in democracies, but in liberal democracies the constitution makers, by the imposition of a complex legislative process, have drastically delimited the range and volume of that voice and blended it with other voices emanating from extraneous, undemocratic sources.

4.

$\mathcal{P}$ARLIAMENTS AS LEGISLATURES IN LIBERAL DEMOCRACIES:

Variations on a Theme

Introduction

Participants in the specialized international congresses that constitute a new routine for scholars are likely, if they are not jurists, to have at least a common subject matter for discussion. Physicians who convene to study diseases are aided in their attempt at mutual understanding by the fact that viruses are international and that the Russian body does not differ significantly from the American body; physicists can be sure that an atom is an atom no matter what state claims sovereignty over it. Jurists and political scientists are less fortunate. Although they seek universal goals in justice and welfare, they do so through intricate, artificial, and unique institutions that virtually defy meaningful comparison.

That this is so may seem at first glance surprising, since the legal mind, ingenious as it is at nice distinctions and sophistic logic, has shown remarkably little originality in setting up states. With few exceptions, the present liberal democratic states are copies of English government as it has been interpreted and misinterpreted through the centuries.[1] Even the relatively startling innovations found in the constitution of France's Fifth Republic are in many instances but another attempt to bring the French government more closely in line with that of the United Kingdom. Parliaments have been no exception to this general rule. The similarity of the models in their formal outlines is deceptive, however, if it leads observers to suppose that comparable epiphenomena are indicative of necessary or even probable similarities in the actual power structure.

Since a legal system is an institution—that is, a work of art and not a product of nature—every nation establishes its own legal concepts and terminology and builds its own state. Each system, each organ, is unique. Furthermore, we are only beginning to understand the complex relationships that link the artificial institution (the state) with the spontaneous group (the nation) and with the countless other groups and institutions, within and without, that bring their pressures to bear on it; and to realize that these relationships are in continuous flux.

Moreover, the same function is often performed by quite different institutions and procedures in different countries. The legislative referendum in Switzerland, for instance, is similar to the private member bill in Great Britain in that they both permit action on matters on which the major parties do not care to take a stand. It is difficult for French-trained students to understand how a government can function effectively without a Conseil d'état, just as it is difficult for an American-trained student to understand how one gets along without judicial review of legislation, or for a British-trained student to see the advantages of either. The truth of the matter is that the essential functions of a Conseil d'état and of judicial review are per-

[1] Mosca suggests that, with the exception of the constitution proposed by Abbé Sieyès and put into effect for two years in France (1800–2), the constitutions *"hanno mostrato più spirito d'imitazione che inventiva"*—Gaetano Mosca, *Teorica dei governi e governo parlamentare* (1887, reprinted in Mosca, *Ciò che potrebbe insegnare la storia* (Milan: Giuffrè, 1958), pp. 17–328 at 158. See also Martin Needler, "On the Dangers of Copying the British," *Political Science Quarterly*, LXXVII (1962), 379–396.

formed, for better or worse, in all three countries. An Italian once told the writer that no democracy could exist in which it would not be a criminal offense to vilify heads of states or heads of important religious sects; he could not conceive of a society such as the American one, where such matters are adequately regulated by canons of taste.

On the other hand, what is ostensibly the same institution may perform quite different functions in different states. There has recently arisen, for instance, a singular fervor in the West for a traditional Swedish institution, the ombudsman, that has resulted in transplanting variants of this element of Swedish government into Norway, Denmark, Great Britain, and New Zealand. It is too early to assess definitively the results of this, but it is safe to say that a comparison between these models and the Swedish original will be rendered difficult and less meaningful than might appear at first sight, not only because of significant differences found in the powers and responsibilities attributed to the ombudsmen but also because of the substantial difference in the social and governmental environments of the various countries in which they are expected to operate.

A comparative study of parliaments is thus a perilous undertaking as soon as it attempts to go beyond an arid confrontation of structures and formal procedures, even though new parliaments are generally copied after earlier ones and parliamentary reforms are often the result of the diffusion of what seemed like a good idea in another system.

It is fortunately, however, not the purpose here to propose a model parliament, a model legislative process, or a panacea for the ills with which present parliaments are beset. All that is called for is a generalized description and criticism of some of the major variations in the structure and procedures of liberal democratic parliaments that have been developed for the purpose of enabling them to function more efficiently as legislatures.

Representation

Parliaments differ in the devices by which they seek to be representative.[2]

The modern way to become a member of parliament is to be elected to that office. We have seen that this was not always so. Yet, regardless of the undemocratic nature of their selection, the medieval parliaments were considered representative. Sir Lewis Namier, moreover, holds that even the pre-1832 rotten borough system represented the national interest in a way that by inference the present parliament does not:

> But while the "political nation" had its proper representation in the knights of the shire and the burgesses of the populous towns, the rotten boroughs formed a reserve of parliamentary seats at the disposal of the strong and of the interested: of the magnates while dominant in the country, of the Court or Crown or Executive, of economic and financial interests as they entered into the balance of forces. That peculiar interplay of influence and independence produced a House representative of the nation, though not of any rationally defined electorate.[3]

The more common view, however, is the classical democratic doctrine of representation expounded by Montesquieu. A free translation and abridgment of his exposition follows:

> Since in a free state every man should govern himself, the legislative power should be in the hands of the people; but since it is impossible to convene the people in a large state and in-

[2] Professor As'ad Rahhal of the University of Wichita prepared the first draft of this section on representation. I regret that circumstances beyond our control made his further assistance on this manuscript unavailable to me.

[3] Lewis B. Namier, "The Elizabethan Parliament," in *Avenues of History* (London: Hamish Hamilton, Ltd., 1952), pp. 103–114 at 104.

convenient to do so even in a small one, it becomes necessary for the people to accomplish through their representatives what they cannot accomplish directly by themselves.

A man knows more about the needs of his own town than about other towns and is a better judge of his neighbors than of strangers; it is therefore fitting that representatives be chosen on a territorial basis.

The great advantage of having representatives is that they are capable of discussing issues, while the people as a whole are not.

It is not necessary that deputies be instructed. It is true that instructed deputies better express the voice of the people, but this system leads to infinite delays and in emergencies the power of the state may be held up indefinitely by a caprice.

Everyone should have the right to vote except those who are in so base a condition as to appear to have no political will.

There should be no direct legislation because whereas the people are capable of choosing deputies, they are not in a position to reach decisions on political matters.[4]

The type of constituency, the residence qualifications of candidates, the nomination procedure, the methods of filling vacancies occurring between elections, and the terms of office of members of parliament—all have an important bearing upon the theory and practice of representation.

Constituencies are based on either territory or function and may be single-member or multi-member. The classical system of territorial representation is based on the single-member district. This system is sometimes criticized as being undemocratic, on the grounds that it does not allow all the interests and groups in society to be equitably represented in parliament. It may result in a significant discrepancy between the popular vote a party receives and the number of parliamentary seats it gains. Thus, when the voting power of a given major party is concentrated in

[4] Charles Louis de Secondat, Baron de la Brède et de Montesquieu, *De l'esprit des lois* (Geneva, 1748). For a general discussion of representation, see Harold Foote Gosnell, *Democracy, the Threshold of Freedom* (New York: The Ronald Press Company, 1948). See also Édouard Bertrand Jouvenel des Ursins, *Arcadie, essais sur le mieux vivre* (Paris: S.E.D.E.I.S., 1968), pp. 66–77.

certain areas and contrasts in this respect with the more even country-wide distribution of votes going to another party, the electoral system produces a bias in favor of the latter, as the first party has to obtain more popular votes than the second one in order to win an equal number of seats. This system is also unfair to minor parties, which are often grossly underrepresented.

Another problem with the single-member district lies in the difficulty of creating and maintaining districts of approximately the same size. In the United States, for example, there have been gross inequalities of representation both in state legislatures and in Congress. The whole system of apportionment favored the rural areas against large urban communities, but as a result of Supreme Court intervention improvement is under way.

In the United Kingdom, there is automatic periodic review of the boundaries of electoral districts for the purpose of keeping them more or less equal in population. A centralized unitary government structure renders such reapportionment easier than it is in the United States, where administration of elections is basically a function of the individual states. Any continuous redrawing of the maps of electoral districts is not, however, without its disadvantages; voters are shifted from one district to another, and party organizations and plans disrupted.

The use of the multi-member district and proportional representation permits equitable representation of the various ideologies and policies propounded by the competing political parties. In its pure form as it operates in the Netherlands and Israel, the state constitutes a single election district and parliament becomes a reflection in miniature of public opinion as expressed by the electorate. Federal systems like Switzerland and Germany use the constituent states as the electoral districts, while Scandinavia and Italy create large territorial units for this purpose.

This model fits the theory of democratic egalitarian representation more closely than does the single-member constituency model. Its disadvantage, however, is that by granting representation to small parties and thus stimulating their proliferation, governments may become unstable coalitions lacking authority and a clearly defined program. This model also tends to loosen the personal ties between elected members and their voters since, rather than choosing a constituency representative to whom he can turn, the voter shows his preference for a party. The successful candidate is one of a group of successful members from one district. Naturally, neither he nor the voters can feel that he represents the whole district as does the representative of a single-member constituency.

In order to counteract the tendency of proportional representation to encourage splinter groups and small parties, various methods that aim at favoring larger parties in the final allocation of seats have been applied in different countries.[5]

Functional representation divides the state for electoral purposes into economic interest groups. In liberal democracies, the representation of interests is left primarily to the pressure groups. This does not mean, however, that certain parties and certain deputies are not known to be the parliamentary spokesmen for various special interests. The rapport between labor interests and socialist parties is close, as is that between Catholic parties and the Roman Catholic Church. In Germany, interest groups have been particularly successful in electing their official representatives to parliament.

Some critics of the legislative process have suggested formalizing functional representation by supplanting territorial with professional or economic representation in at least one house of parliament. This proposal, which was suggested by Adam Müller and Hegel, and was later expounded by the French Catholic theorists,[6] would appear to have the advantage of incorporating some of the major pressure groups within the formal structure of the state and thus giving legal status to the representatives of a number of important social forces within society. For this reason among others, such representation was favored by the

---

[5] For a general discussion, see Douglas Rae, *The Political Consequences of Electoral Laws* (New Haven, Conn., Yale University Press, 1967).

[6] See René Charles Humbert, Marquis de la Tour du Pin Chambly de La Charce, *Vers un ordre social chrétien, Jalons de route 1882–1907* (6th ed., Paris: Beauchesne, 1942); Charles Benoist, *La crise de l'état moderne* (Paris: Firmin-Didot, 1897); and John Clarke Adams, "Some Antecedents of the Theory of the Corporate System," *Journal of the History of Ideas,* III (1942), 182–189.

Syndicalists and Guild Socialists, as well as by some of the Fabians such as Sidney and Beatrice Webb, who proposed the establishment of a political parliament on the one hand and a social and economic parliament on the other.[7] Functional representation received the kiss of death, however, when Catholic and fascist theorists combined to make the corporate system an adjunct of fascism.[8]

An interesting variant of functional representation was advocated by Gaetano Mosca. Mosca held that the upper house of parliament as generally constituted represented anachronistic eighteenth-century classes and interests, which did not represent the true interests of the nation, and that it was consequently an improper means of restraining the popularly elected lower house. He proposed to replace such an upper house with one that would represent the vital and active social interests of the future. Members of his upper house would be chosen by the various classes of workers. In each province, three categories of electors would be set up. The first would consist of all the university graduates resident in the province; the second, of representatives of the middle-class workers who had completed their secondary school education. The third would include representatives of those manual laborers who could read and write and who were organized into unions maintaining minimum standards of seriousness of purpose and were on this score recognized by the state. This body of electors would elect the number of senators assigned to the province.[9]

[7] For a favorable account, see G. D. H. Cole, *Guild Socialism: A Plan for Economic Democracy* (New York: Frederick A. Stokes Co., 1921). For an unfavorable one, see C. E. M. Joad, *Introduction to Modern Political Theory* (London: Oxford University Press, 1924).

[8] See Alfredo Rocco, "Crisi dello stato e sindacati," *Politica*, VII (1920), 1–14, and Gabriele D'Annunzio di Montenevoso, "Carta della reggenza del Carnaro," in D'Annunzio, *Per la più grande Italia* (Milan: Istituto nazionale per le edizioni di tutte le opere di Gabriele D'Annunzio, 1932). For the argument that the corporate system tends inevitably to tyranny, see Gaëtan Pirou, *Essais sur le corporatisme* (Paris: Félix Alcan, 1938).

[9] Gaetano Mosca, *Le costituzioni moderne* (1887), reprinted in Mosca, *Ciò che potrebbe insegnare la storia*, pp. 443–590 at 538–543. See also Mosca, *Teorica*, ch. 6, sec. 5.

Functional representation was proposed by Pierre Mendès-France in his project for a replacement for the Fifth French Republic. Closely following Mosca's reasoning on the obsolete bases of present upper chambers, Mendès-France proposed the creation of an upper chamber based on socioeconomic representation, where representatives of the diverse socioeconomic groups would confront each other and reach decisions in the mutual interest. This house would operate alongside a national assembly elected by universal adult suffrage, where the political aspirations and beliefs of every Frenchman would be represented.[10]

Ireland is the only liberal democratic state that formally elects one house of parliament on a functional basis. There, the upper house is elected by the members of the lower house and members of the local councils from among panels of nominees representing cultural and economic interests.[11] Both Italy and France have something like third chambers on economic matters, on which only consultative powers are bestowed. The Consiglio nazionale dell'economia e del lavoro is a body of 80 members, of whom 59 represent the various economic interests within the nation. The trade unions designate their own representatives; others are appointed by the president.[12] All bills of a general nature that affect economic interests directly are referred to the Consiglio. The Consiglio, which operates on a level about midway between a British Royal Commission and a normal parliamentary standing committee, gives its advice on the bill and frequently makes counterproposals; it has not performed miracles, but is generally considered to have proven itself a useful adjunct to parliamentary government.

[10] Pierre Mendès-France, *La république moderne* (Paris: Gallimard, 1962), pp. 91–97.

[11] My colleague, Professor Frank Munger, informs me that in practice (1) the upper chamber of the Dail is for the most part, like the Canadian Senate, an old politicians' home; (2) it does not in effect represent economic and cultural interests; and (3) its most distinguished members are in good part the independent-minded representatives of the Irish universities.

[12] Paolo Barile, *Corso di diritto costituzionale* (Padua: CEDAM, 1962), pp. 132–133.

The Conseil économique et social of the Fifth Republic is more of a technical advisory board than a functional assembly. It meets only at the request of the government and its meetings are secret. Unlike its Italian counterpart, it has no power of initiative. The Conseil has 205 members, about a third of whom are chosen by the government.

These French and Italian councils were both the result of Roman Catholic pressure in favor of an upper house based on functional representation. The compromise reached with the powerful Communist and Socialist parties in the constituent assemblies was the establishment of these advisory councils.

Although functional representation has been formally instituted only in Roman Catholic countries,[13] and among democracies only in Ireland, there is considerable informal functional representation in most democratic parliaments; correspondingly, territorial representation is becoming less important. The result of interest representation in parliament is to reduce the role in parliament of the statesman *au-dessus de la mêlée,* and to increase the role of the agent; to decrease the prestige of parliament derived from the excellence of its members, and to substitute another prestige garnered from the power and importance of the interests represented. Thus, to the degree that functional representation becomes the pattern—however informally it may impose itself—the Burkeian image of the statesman aristocrat, which is still the image of the British Conservative Party,[14] is declining, to be replaced by the essentially anonymous agent of an interest.[15]

[13] For Spain and Portugal, see "A organização e o funcionamento do poder legislativo," *Revista do serviço publico,* LXXVII (1957), 149–394 at 246–268.

[14] See Sir Ivor Jennings, *British Political Parties* (3 vols., Vol. II, Cambridge: Cambridge University Press, 1961), Vol. II, pp. 344–345; and Quintin Hogg, *The Case for Conservatism* (Harmondsworth, Middlesex: Penguin Books, 1947), *passim.*

[15] A minor scandal arose in Great Britain in 1966 over a blatant instance of interest representation in the British parliament. The Hon. Frank Cousins, a Labour MP and former Minister of Technology, entered into an agreement with the Transport and General Workers' Union by which Cousins, the general secretary of the union, agreed to accept his full salary

In most European countries, candidates are not legally required to be residents of the districts in which they are elected,[16]
the importance of political parties making this possible. Generally speaking, the abolition of residence requirements for members of parliaments in Europe is recent. The United States constitution provides for residential requirements for both representatives and senators[17]; similar requirements are also found in
the constitutions of the various states. In practice, this rule has
been carried even further, and it is now often difficult for a person who is not a native or at least a long-established resident in
an electoral district to be elected there, even if he meets the
legal requirements of residence. The election of Senator Robert
Kennedy in New York must be considered a notable exception
in this respect and may reflect a new trend developing out of
the increasing homogeneity and mobility of the population. In
spite of the general absence of residence requirements in the
European continent, however, regional sentiment tends to have
the same effect as the legal requirements in the United States
or the Scandinavian countries. Strong parties may counteract
this sense of localism: in Italy, for example, the parties often
nominate their leading candidates in three districts—the maximum permitted by the law. Thus the *capolista* (the candidate
placed at the top of the list), who lends his national prestige to
the local list, is frequently an outsider, while all but the few
top names are of only local significance.

The increasing importance of the role of political parties in

---

as general secretary while in the House of Commons (apparently turning
over his smaller parliamentary salary to the union). In that house he would
then be expected to play a major part in the opposition to the Profits and
Incomes Bill. "The member for Nuneaton, in other words, is staying in
Parliament at the behest of his employer [the union] and in order to further his employer's aims." Thus the "people of Nuneaton, who pay Mr.
Cousins to represent them at Westminster, are to get a smaller share of his
time and attention." The quotes are from an editorial in the *Manchester
Guardian Weekly* of July 14, 1966, p. 1.

[16] Sweden is an exception here, with respect to the Andra Kammar.

[17] Article I, sec. 2, cl. 2, and Article I, sec. 3, cl. 3.

representation can also be seen in the methods of choosing candidates. The independent candidate, nominating himself and seeking the support of the voters on his own, is becoming a rarity. In most European countries, the party organizations themselves choose the candidates; the main question relevant to representation here is the degree to which local party organizations can influence this choice. Generally speaking, the stronger the discipline and the centralization of the party, the greater the role of national leadership in determining candidates to run in the various districts. In the United Kingdom, nevertheless, local party organizations play an important role in the choice of parliamentary candidates, although their nominations must win the endorsement of the central party machinery. The local party members also have some influence because the candidates chosen by the local executive committee are normally presented for approval by a general meeting of the local members. The role of the party agent during the elections and between election campaigns is crucial, and gives a further illustration that elections in the United Kingdom are almost exclusively a party function.

In Sweden, local party organizations play a still more important role in the nomination of candidates than do their British counterparts. The principle of central approval of locally chosen candidates has not gained much ground there. Nomination meetings are held locally, in which party members may propose candidates and express their opinions; the responsibility for drafting the final list of party candidates, however, remains in the hands of the party leadership in the constituency. Sometimes the same party prepares different lists for various parts of the electoral constituency, in order to suit the party nominees to the particular needs and interests of different localities.

Switzerland is one of the few countries where local considerations still outweigh party affiliation. In forming their lists, the national parties, which are (with the exception of the Socialists), little more than coalitions of cantonal parties, must pay special attention to the particular situations and interests in the various cantons. And although candidature must be on the basis of party lists, the freedom of choice of the parties is limited by the fact that a large number of voters do not vote on the basis of a straight party ticket; *panachage* (split ticket voting) is permitted and frequently resorted to by the Swiss. Thus parties take care to include on their lists persons who are locally attractive. For the same purpose, Swiss parties often resort to a practice similar to the Swedish one of putting up several different lists to meet the particular needs of different districts within larger cantons (the canton, irrespective of size, is the electoral constituency).

The French Fifth Republic has dropped the system of proportional representation of the Fourth Republic and returned to the Third Republic practice of single-member constituencies with *ballottage,* a system requiring a second election if no candidate gets a majority in the first. In the second election, a plurality is sufficient to win. In the French system, unlike the system of runoff elections held in some Southern states in the United States, the second election for the parliament is not limited to the two candidates who received the most votes on the first ballot. No person may run on the second ballot, however, unless he was already a candidate on the first and obtained at least 5 per cent of the votes.

Although political parties, as we have seen, play the determinant role in the selection of candidates for elections in most European democracies, their activities are not recognized legally as part of the formal state machinery. But West Germany and Norway are notable exceptions in this regard. The German 1956 electoral law gives the local party organizations the *exclusive* right of nominating candidates for the national elections. Party conventions, composed of locally elected delegates, are held in each land for nominating the list of candidates and in each constituency for nominating the single-member district candidates. Central party organizations try to (and indeed, do) exercise influence on their local branches, but the final word, *de iure* and *de facto,* rests with the local people. In making their selections, especially for candidates in single-member constituencies, the local party organizations pay special attention to local considerations, with an eye to choosing those candidates who can best attract the popular votes in the district; they try to form a "balanced," list in which the various local interests prevailing in the Land are represented.[18] This tends to bring to the Bundestag persons belonging to the various interests and professions, thus contributing to the general representativeness of this assembly. The majority of voters seem to select party designations rather than individual personalities; consequently, it is rare for a voter to cast his vote for a single-member constituency candidate of a party different from that for whose Land list he voted. This strict party conformity may be, however, partially misleading. The average German voter prefers to vote a straight party ticket; but it must be remembered that the care with which the party organizations choose their local candidates encourages him in his preference.

By statutory provision, the Norwegian parties are empowered to hold local conventions for the nomination of the party candidates in the various electoral districts. Although this practice is not mandatory, party conventions are a legally recognized formal institution subsidized by the state, which pays the expenses of all the official delegates to these conventions. Here the Norwegian practice comes nearest to the American party conventions and primaries. The main difference is that the American primaries are directly administered by the regular election officers, with all costs paid from the public treasury.

Direct primaries have been introduced in the United States for the purpose of reducing the influence of the party caucuses and giving the individual citizen the right to participate in the selection of candidates. Party organizations, however, still play the dominant role in the selection of candidates; that of the voters is normally limited to approving the choices of the party leadership. The importance of direct primaries is that they facilitate popular control of the parties when the public decides to take this responsibility.

A by-election (from the Norwegian by meaning town) is a special election in a single constituency. By-elections are the method employed for filling vacancies in the United Kingdom,

[18] This tendency is not limited to Germany. In general, the representation of the various functional interests in the electoral district tends to carry more weight than merely territorial considerations in the choice of candidates for the proportional representation party lists.

the United States, and most countries having single-member constituencies. They allow the voters to express their will in the light of changing circumstances, if any, and they are often a valuable indicator of shifts in public opinion between elections. In the Fifth French Republic and in Belgium, electors vote simultaneously for an original candidate and a substitute, who would replace the original deputy in case of the latter's death, resignation, or acceptance of a position incompatible with membership in parliament (such as a ministerial position in France, for example). By-elections take place only if the substitute becomes unavailable. Voters can have no choice in the election of a substitute. Each candidate designates his substitute and the two names appear together on the ballot; whoever votes for the original candidate votes automatically for his substitute as well. A situation can arise where the voter likes the candidate but not the substitute, or vice versa, but he can do nothing about it. The fact that party affiliation is the preponderant element in the choice the voter makes tends, however, to reduce the frequency of such conflicts. The French have not yet established a conventional behavior for the alternate who replaces a deputy who accepts a position in the government and later resigns or is forced out of office. The majority of alternates under these circumstances resign their seats, thus giving the former ministers the chance to return to parliament via a by-election. Maurice Couve de Murville's alternate, however, refused to resign in 1969 and Couve was forced to run in another constituency, whose representative was more accommodating. In the ensuing by-election, the voters rejected de Gaulle's former prime minister and elected the candidate of a splinter socialist party instead.

For elections to the Riksdag in Sweden, a system of alternates is optional with the parties: if adopted, the party places the names of two alternates after the name of each candidate. If all three become incapacitated, the seat goes to the next man on the list and then to his alternates.[19] The situation facing the French, the Belgian, and occasionally the Swedish voter is in a

---

[19] Andrén, *op. cit.*, pp. 51, 53.

way similar to that facing the American voter in the election of the vice president.[20] Whereas in the French and Belgian systems the alternate substitutes for a specific member and is seated only on the death, expulsion, or resignation of the deputy, the Norwegian method is to elect *varamenn* (alternates), who substitute indiscriminately for any party representative from a multi-member constituency. A varamann, moreover, is empowered to replace a deputy on a temporary as well as a permanent basis. He thus may sit and vote for a deputy who is ill or who is occupied (e.g., on a diplomatic mission, with committee work, on vacation, in electioneering). The varamenn are the next in line for election on the party election lists. The number of varamenn elected for each party from each district is two more than the number of members of the Storting elected by that party from that district. Thus if enough votes are cast to elect three men, the three candidates with the highest number of preference votes will become regular members of the Storting and the next five will become varamenn.[21] The system of the varamann is a general Norwegian practice and is used in social and business organizations as well as in the government. The main example of this practice in American politics is the alternate at a presidential convention. Alternates are also elected to the standing committees of the Bundestag.

The general rule for filling parliamentary vacancies in states using proportional representation is to give the vacant seat to the candidate of the same party and electoral district highest on the party list among the men elected. Where preference voting is permitted, it goes to the candidate highest in preference votes among the men not elected. This method is followed in Italy, the Netherlands, Switzerland, and West Germany. It also avoids by-elections, and tends to keep party representation in parliament constant throughout the whole parliamentary term.

[20] The voter in the State of New York is also in a similar situation: there a single vote is cast for the governor and the lieutenant governor.

[21] See James Storing, *Norwegian Democracy* (Boston: Houghton Mifflin Company, 1963), pp. 67–69.

Vacancies occurring in the United States Senate are normally filled by means of temporary appointments by state governors. This procedure is based on the provision of the Seventeenth Amendment stating that ". . . the legislature of any State may empower the executive thereof to make temporary appointments until the people fill the vacancies by elections as the legislature may direct." As a rule, by-elections for the remainder of a regular six-year Senate term are held simultaneously with the regular biennial national elections, and the appointees are very often reelected, the voters thus endorsing the choice originally made by their governor.

Vacancies occurring among the five life posts in the Italian Senate are filled by presidential appointment; members of the Canadian Senate are appointed for life by the governor general on the advice of the prime minister; when accession to the House of Lords is neither by birthright nor *ex officio,* it is by appointment. In a sense, in each of these cases one can speak of an indirect election, as the president of Italy is elected by persons directly elected by the public, and the same can be said for the British cabinet, which appoints the new Lords.

One of the factors that contributes to the responsiveness of elected persons, and hence to their representativeness, is their interest in being reelected. Thus the shorter the term of office of elected bodies, the greater the degree of responsiveness of their members to the needs and opinions of the electorate. This is a major justification of the American practice of two-year terms on both the state and the federal levels. In view of the complexity of modern government, however, and of the long-range character of most important government policies, excessively short terms of office are not desirable. Legislators need time to acquire the knowledge and experience to follow up the policies and programs they have authorized. Overlong terms, on the other hand, may create a gulf between the legislators and the climate of opinion among the electorate. A member who finds himself secure in office for a long period of time may be tempted to ignore the interests of his constituents or even to act against these interests.

As a compromise solution, many countries have adopted parliamentary terms of from four to five years, on the assumption that this gives the representatives sufficient time to carry out government programs, while giving the electorate sufficient opportunity for expressing their opinion. Thus the three- and two-year terms respectively of the Australian and American Houses of Representatives are too short by generally accepted standards. (The annual election of the two representatives of St. Gallen to the Swiss Conseil des états is merely a formal periodic affirmation of confidence, voted not by the general electorate but by the cantonal legislature.)

Many essays on the representative nature of parliament begin with the polemical statements in Edmund Burke's address to the electors of Bristol in 1774, when the eminent statesman said: "Your representative owes you not his industry only, but his judgment, and he betrays, instead of serving you, if he sacrifices it to your opinion." [22] The principle that a member of parliament represents the whole nation and not a particular district has won wide acceptance, and many modern constitutions include articles embodying this principle. Also related to this are the frequently met constitutional provisions making mandates binding on the elected members illegal. No one has stated the case more clearly than Walter Bagehot. A century ago he understood the difference between the fanatical, intolerant, dedicated party hack and the sober, experienced broker statesman at Westminster:

> Constituency government is the precise opposite of parliamentary government. It is the government of immoderate persons far from the scene of action, instead of the government of moderate persons close to the scene of action; it is the judgment of persons judging in the last resort and without penalty, in lieu of persons judging in fear of a dissolution, and ever conscious that they are subject to an appeal.[23]

[22] *The Works of Edmund Burke* (Boston: Little, Brown & Co., 1897), cited in Howard A. Hamilton (ed.), *Political Institutions* (Boston: Houghton Mifflin Company, 1962), p. 181.

[23] Walter Bagehot, *The English Constitution* (1867), ch. V, para. 23.

A contemporary Australian politician, on being asked: "Do you think that the Member of Parliament is responsible to the pulse of his electorate?" replied:

> I have been too long in politics to take that position seriously. . . . A man is elected. . . . He takes up his quarters in what, after all, are very comfortable surroundings and the atmosphere which he breathes day and night is the atmosphere of men like himself, and the other atmosphere of Canberra, of public servants and a few score traders. He may be propelled from his electorate charged with the feelings of his constituents, but the charge is dissipated long before he has been a week in Canberra. You have to breathe the air daily. We are all responsive to our daily surroundings.[24]

The tendency to consider the representatives as agents, though not new (cf., in Chapter 2, the *mandat impératif* that hamstrung the États généraux), has increased with the decreased humility of the electorate and its greater interest in and concern for legislation. The controversy over the presumed conflict between these positions has actually little meaning. Politics is a profession and politicians in general want to be reelected.[25] If there is, therefore, a discernible constituent opinion on an issue that will presumably still be live at the time of the next election, and if in the meantime there is no reason to expect a *volte face* of constituent opinion on that issue, a representative will need great moral courage (or a serious disregard for his reelection) to thwart the will of his constituents. Casting all theories aside, to this degree professional politicians are in practice agents. But in the majority of cases, where there is no discernible constituent opinion, the professional politician is free to vote as he chooses. In any case, his concern for his constituents' opinion is

---

[24] Quoted in Leslie Finley Crisp, *The Parliamentary Government of Australia* (3rd ed., London: Longmans, Green & Co., Ltd., 1961), p. 63.

[25] "It is a pretty poor Congressman who cannot convince himself that the best interests of the public depend on his reelection"—D. W. Brogan, *An Introduction to American Politics* (London: Hamish Hamilton, Ltd., 1954), p. 350.

not for what it may be on the day he votes but rather for what it will be on the day they vote.[26]

This is not to say that there do not arise in the careers of most representatives, and certainly of all who deserve to be called statesmen, moments of conflict between the mandate of the informed conscience of the representative and the poorly informed emotional response of his electorate. A number of "dove" senators who as chance decreed came up for reelection in 1968 were beset by just such a conflict. Obviously they wanted to have their cake and eat it, too, and thus were led to indulge in what Professor Berman calls "strategic obfuscation." [27] If they are blamed for being less than candid, they may reply that a slightly soiled dove with a vote in the Senate is more valuable to the nation than a lily-white dove with no vote. The kingdom of Jesus is not of this earth and the path of the pristine rarely leads to political office.

One of the purposes of representation is to reduce the unwieldy dimensions of an assembly of all the citizens to a size commensurate with effective deliberation. Weighed against this principle is the one that holds there is a maximum number of people a single representative can represent equitably.[28] Modern techniques have not altered the optimum size of legislatures, but they have noticeably increased the effective size of constituencies. Traditionally, the member of the lower house of parliament representing a single-member constituency was considered the backbone of the representative system. The tendency in the

[26] For a number of statements by American politicians holding the free agent (trustee) or agent (delegate) position, see George Blair, *American Legislatures: Structure and Process* (New York: Harper & Row, 1967), pp. 110–116. On the general question, see John C. Wahlke, Heinz Eulau, William Buchanan, and Leroy Ferguson, *The Legislative System: Explorations in Legislative Behavior* (New York: John Wiley, 1962), chs. 12 and 13; and Wilder W. Crane, Jr., "Do Representatives Represent?", *Journal of Politics*, XXII (1960), 295–299. For an excellent summary of the American practice, see Daniel M. Berman, *In Congress Assembled* (New York: The Macmillan Company, 1964), pp. 48–60.

[27] *Op. cit.*, p. 48.

[28] For a classical exposition of this dilemma, see *The Federalist*, No. X (Madison).

modern world is away from localism, from neighborliness. There is greater social mobility than ever before, less local homogeneity, and far less economic and social self-sufficiency in local groups. Even gossip, which used to be eminently local, is now centered on Hollywood, Washington, and New York. The silly women who used to pry into their neighbors' lives now read the columnists and seek to supplement their meager emotional sustenance by entering vicariously into the daily and particularly nightly lives of the élite. The result of all this is a decrease in the cohesion of the local territorial group and a consequent decrease in interest in and rapport with the local congressman.

The advent of proportional representation has eliminated the figure of the constituency representative from much of Europe (he still exists in France, Germany, and the small Swiss cantons). And over the liberal democratic world—thanks to the television and radio networks, national newspaper coverage, and the advertising techniques employed by the top national political personalities—the voter identifies with and considers himself represented by the national party leaders rather than by his constituency representative. The politically conscious voter in the United States follows the policy of his President and perhaps of his senators. He writes them letters on occasion and tends to hold them responsible for their decisions, but he is likely to consider his congressman too far down in the political pecking order to matter very much. The same can be said for many European countries, where it is the national political figures who seek and attract masses of voters, the local politicians tending to represent factional interests. Once it was hard to know much about national leaders, but then one did know more about one's neighbors than today. Thus it was expected that the voters would be in a particularly good position to pick good congressmen. Today, constituencies are so large that the congressman is no longer known to most of his constituents. Although the voter can know little more about the real president of the United States than did the voters of a century ago, he is well aware of the image of national political leaders created by the advertising and theatrical world. Only when a political leader forgets he is on stage and clamorously steps out of the part do we perceive a human being, as when Harry Truman castigated a music critic who was unfavorably impressed by his daughter's singing, or when Lyndon Johnson picked up a dog by the ears.

Image building is not a new political trick. As in certain other aspects of modern life, the novelty of today's political image building lies only in the magnitude of the enterprise. The Republicans successfully created an image partially to conceal the lacunae in Calvin Coolidge, but they didn't use Hollywood and Madison Avenue to do it. Dwight Eisenhower was among the first political figures to hire an actor as a coach. It took Hollywood less than a generation to realize the implications of this and elect George Murphy and Ronald Reagan directly to high public office.

With the advent of strong national parties and articulate and persuasive pressure groups, territorial representation lost some of its prestige and importance. "Party," as Sir Ivor Jennings has said, "is a complex idea which . . . like Topsy and the British Constitution, just growed" [29]; but the influence on the parliamentary system of this unwanted, unexpected, and ubiquitous intruder can hardly be overestimated. As Duverger has written:

> He who is learned in constitutional law and is ignorant of the function of party in the political process cannot understand modern political regimes; he who understands the function of party and is ignorant of constitutional law has an incomplete but exact idea of modern political regimes. [30]

When widely representative governments were first established, political parties as we know them did not exist. What did exist were factions, a phenomenon as old as human society. Liberal democratic theorists were generally opposed to factions, and men with particularly intuitive insight into the future work-

[29] *British Political Parties* (3 vols., Cambridge: Cambridge University Press, 1961), Vol. II, p. 3.

[30] Maurice Duverger, *Les partis politiques* (Paris: A. Colin, 1951), p. 388. (Author's translation.)

ings of democracy, such as Harrington and Rousseau, insisted on the necessity of eliminating all expressions of factional interests in parliament.

The true political party, an organization designed for the purpose of winning elections where there exists an extended suffrage, is an American invention. Hamilton and Adams, although factious men, were by natural inclination too aristocratic to favor the introduction into politics of anything so essentially vulgar as a party machine. Jefferson, their antagonist, who did not share these scruples, created the political party, an institution that has spread over the world and revolutionized the political process.

The political party developed in Great Britain after the Reform Acts of 1832 and 1867, as the Whig and Tory factions gradually transformed themselves into the Liberal and Conservative parties. On the continent, the parliamentary factions of the French Revolution, such as the Jacobins, the Girondins, and the Montagnards, were perhaps embryonic parties even before Jefferson created the Democratic Republican Party; but the true party did not appear there until the latter half of the nineteenth century.

The Anglo-American attitude toward party gradually shifted from one of hostility to one of reluctant acceptance and later to the presently held opinion of many scholars that parties are positively beneficial. Even an early Whig like Daniel Webster expressed a grudging toleration of party. "The existence of parties in popular government is not to be avoided, and if they are formed on constitutional questions, or in regard to great measures of public policy, and do not run to excessive lengths, it may be admitted that on the whole they do no great harm." [31]

Walter Bagehot was one of the first Englishmen to assess correctly the beneficent effect of party on parliament, seeing that party was the basis of parliamentary organization and that without organization parliament would be helpless.[32] By the turn of

---

[31] *Congressional Debates*, IX, p. 459, cited in Charles Edward Merriam, *American Political Ideas* (New York: The Macmillan Company, 1920), p. 272.

[32] Bagehot, *The English Constitution*, esp. ch. V, paras. 17–18. It is imma-

the century it had become more common to speak well of parties. Ostrogorski, writing of the United States, was one of the first to believe that the parties were not only inevitable but a potential good.[33] Benoist, thinking primarily of France, came to a similar conclusion, recognizing the necessity of parties and considering their presence a sign of the strength rather than the weakness of the parliamentary system.[34] Today, many distinguished American political scientists (reacting against the anti-party attitudes of the reformers earlier in the century) reach the conclusion that the weakness, not the strength, of American parties is impeding the proper function of representative government in the United States.[35]

A member of parliament who is also a member of a national political party can now feel that he represents an interest that is national rather than merely local. And the greater the coherence, discipline, and militancy of the party, the greater this feeling. A member's destiny is increasingly being tied up with his party rather than with his constituency. This is more obviously so in Europe, where a system of proportional representation, or the British tradition of not requiring residence in the constituency

---

terial to his argument (and ours) that Bagehot does not distinguish between party and faction.

[33] Moisei Iakoflovich Ostrogorski, *Democracy and the Organization of Political Parties* (New York: The Macmillan Company, 1908).

[34] "Ne croyez point . . . que les partis politiques soient une faiblesse et une maladie de l'État moderne. Ils sont au contraire la condition et le signe d'une vie politique forte"—Charles Benoist, "Le parti," *Revue des deux mondes* (1904), reprinted in Benoist, *Les maladies*, p. 157.

"En France il est bien impossible que nous eussions le régime parlementaire puisque sauf de très rares et très courtes exceptions nous n'avons jamais eu de partis"—Benoist, *Les maladies*, pp. 28–29.

[35] See, for example, *Toward a More Responsible Party System*, American Political Science Association; Berman, *op. cit.*, especially pp. 400–405; Robert G. Spivack, "Bourbons, Bosses, and Brokers," *The Nation*, April 30, 1960, pp. 381–383, reprinted in Hamilton, *op. cit.*, pp. 121–123; and the writings of E. E. Schattschneider, James McGregor Burns, and Stephen K. Bailey. Robert A. Goodwin (ed.), *Political Parties USA* (Chicago: Rand McNally & Co., 1964), presents the varying views of this question in the words of Bailey, Edward C. Banfield, and Walter Berns, pp. 1–58.

one represents, gives a candidate a wide choice of seats to contest. It is also true in America, in that the party can usually find an appointive position for the unsuccessful candidate who is considered a useful and loyal party man, thus freeing him somewhat from the whims of the electors of a given constituency.

In spite of the diatribes written against the party boss, the attempts by Marxist parties, particularly in the early years of their formation, to hold their parliamentary group strictly accountable to the party hierarchy, and the right-wing groups whose votes in parliament may be controlled by a vested interest (for example, the Comité des forges in the French Third Republic, or the Roman Catholic Church), the truth of the matter is that the parties operate in and through parliament and strengthen rather than weaken parliamentary prestige and responsibility.

From the viewpoint of organization, the political party is a monster. On the one hand, it is composed of a normal pyramidal structure leading from the local units to the national executive. Added to this is the irrational appendage of the parliamentary group, composed of the men the party has succeeded in electing to office. It is simple for the party hierarchs to consider these representatives pawns controlled by an extra-parliamentary general staff. It usually does not work that way, however. Occasionally, there appears behind the political scene a true *éminence grise* who operates by pulling strings out of view. Usually, however, it is the representatives, the men in the public eye, the vote-getters, the *divi* of politics, as it were, who do the dictating. Many parties give formal acknowledgment of the power of these *divi* by the dominant role they assign to the parliamentary group in the party executive. Regardless of its formal position in the party, however, the role of the parliamentary group in the formation of party policy is generally so great that the party can be considered as a gain rather than a loss for parliamentary government.

About the time the general public in liberal democracies understood the usefulness and necessity of political parties, pressure groups became the major object of irrational invective. As Professor Rose has remarked, however, "Parties and pressure groups are not independent, as conventional terminology implies. Both are parts of a single political system." [36] Pressure groups are a form of faction probably as old as social groups. But the techniques that modern pressure groups employ are new, and the omnipresence of modern government has significantly increased their number and the scope of their activity.[37] Pressure groups foster the political aims of a specific interest group. They arise when interest groups are not satisfied with the political support

[36] Richard Rose, Politics in England (Boston: Little, Brown & Co., 1964), p. 127.

[37] The literature on pressure groups is voluminous. Early works of interest include Arthur F. Bentley, The Process of Government (Indianapolis: The Bobbs-Merrill Co., Inc., 1908); Lincoln Steffens, The Autobiography of Lincoln Steffens (New York: Harcourt, Brace, 1931), Part III; Peter H. Odegard, Pressure Politics: The Story of the Anti-Saloon League (New York: Columbia University Press, 1928); and Alfred de Grazia, Public and Republic (New York: Alfred A. Knopf, Inc., 1951). A large portion of the case studies, such as those of the Inter-University Case Study Program edited by Edwin Bock, are firsthand studies of pressure groups and pressure politics. Abraham Holtzman, Interest Groups and Lobbying (New York: The Macmillan Company, 1966), is an excellent primer in comparative lobbies. See also Henry W. Ehrmann (ed.), Interest Groups on Four Continents (Pittsburgh, Pa.: University of Pittsburgh Press, 1958). For Great Britain, see S. E. Finer, Autonomous Empire (2d ed., London: Pall Mall Press, 1966); Henry Eckstein, Pressure Group Politics (London: Allen & Unwin, Ltd., 1960); J. D. Stewart, British Pressure Groups (London: Oxford University Press, 1958); R. T. McKenzie, "Parties, Pressure Groups, and the British Political Process," Political Quarterly, XXIX (1958), 5–16; Samuel H. Beer, "Pressure Groups and Parties in Britain," American Political Science Review, L (1956), 1–23; and Samuel H. Beer, "The Representation of Interests in British Government," American Political Science Review, LI (1957), 613–650. For Italy, see Joseph LaPalombara, Interest Groups in Italian Politics (Princeton, N.J.: Princeton University Press, 1964). For France, see Jean Meynaud, Les groupes de pression en France (Paris: A. Colin, 1958); Bernard E. Brown, "Alcohol and Politics in France," American Political Science Review, LI (1957), 976–994; and Bernard E. Brown, "Pressure Politics in the Fifth Republic," Journal of Politics, XXV (1963), 509–525. For a comparative study of political tactics of a single interest group, see Walter Galenson, Trade Union Democracy in Western Europe (Berkeley, Calif.: University of California Press, 1961). The German trade union movement, not treated in the Galenson book, is discussed in John Huddleston, "Trade Unions in the German Federal Republic," Political Quarterly, XXXVIII (1967), 165–176.

they are getting. They operate at all levels of government, choosing in each case the point in the governmental process that best combines the qualities of having effective power and being susceptible to the particular pressure the group can bring to bear. The techniques of pressure groups vary markedly according to the political structures and traditions of the different countries. The loose party system in the United States, and the power of the congressional committees and independent regulatory commissions, peculiar to the United States, have caused American pressure groups to direct particular attention to the committees and the commissions. In Great Britain, the existence of strong parties tends to concentrate pressure on the cabinet and the executive departments, with the backbencher taking a back seat. The German and Italian habit of direct parliamentary representation of major pressure groups tends to merge pressure politics and parliament.

The picture of the nefarious lobbyist passing bribes to members of parliament is still a popular myth. There are at least two reasons why it is not a general practice. One is that lobbyists and representatives are likely to have a sense of ethics (or a fear of being caught); the other, that they are still more likely to have a little common sense. Good lobbyists don't buy votes outright. They give information and contribute to political campaigns, and representatives are in need of information and sources of campaign funds.

A good pressure group is not content merely to publicize opinions; it must also offer solutions. In his letters to his constituents, Clem Miller cited the case of two economic groups, the walnut growers and the chicken farmers, who were in financial difficulties as a result of overproduction. Because the walnut growers were well organized and were represented by an effective pressure group that came up with a positive program, they got help from Congress. The chicken farmers, a larger and therefore potentially more powerful group, were poorly organized and consequently got nothing.[38] Legislators obviously lack the time

[38] Clem Miller, *Member of the House* (New York: Charles Scribner's Sons, 1961), pp. 137–140.

and often the expertise or inclination to study the problems of a depressed group and come up with a reasonable answer. Legislators partake of the divinity in that they too are prone to help those who help themselves. Inasmuch as they represent valid interests—and this is almost always the case—pressure groups parallel and supplement the representative function of parliament. They serve the same democratic end to the degree that they help effectuate popular control over the executives; and they complement the function of parliament in their direct dealings with that body, in that they supply the members of parliament with valuable advice and information.

In those states in which the chief executive is popularly elected, parliament loses the exclusive claim of being the authoritative voice of the people. In this respect, it was once fashionable and proper to distinguish between parliamentary and presidential systems and to maintain that only the latter had popularly elected executives. The truth of the matter is that in most well-established parliamentary systems (e.g., Australia, Canada, Denmark, Great Britain, New Zealand, Norway, and Sweden), the voter in a general election is electing the prime minister just as directly as he is when voting for members of the electoral college in the United States. The significant difference between the systems is that in parliamentary government the representative natures of the legislature and the executive are commingled, and in the presidential systems the two organs are likely to be less well coordinated. In either case, the publicity and prestige connected with the office of the chief executive keep him increasingly in the public eye, and Madison Avenue and Hollywood (or their foreign equivalents) encourage the electors to identify with him rather than with the local constituency representative.

A recent competitor with parliament as the representative of *vox populi* is the opinion poll. The predictions of what millions think, based on how hundreds react, merit the serious attention of politicians, but if the polls really did the job some believe they do, it might be possible to dispense with representative democracy altogether. Human beings, however, are—among other things—irrational, fickle, and ornery, and as such their passions, reasoning, and actions are eminently unpredictable. So the polls remain not a substitute for the politician but merely an aid to him in his dual role of forming policy and interpreting public opinion. But since good polling services cost money, it is usually chief executives and major parties rather than independent parliamentarians who can afford to use them.

Strong parties, powerful pressure groups operating in and out of parliament, and active chief executives with direct lines of communication to the electorate are thus not necessarily inimical to the continuance of a respected and responsible parliament. As in many other cases, potential rivalry—a condition that superficially suggests duplication of effort and open antagonism—may be conducive under enlightened leadership to fruitful collaboration. An equilibrium between competing representative bodies, and a coordination of the activities, becomes essential to the persistence of liberal democratic government; the elimination or even a significant overall diminution of the part played by executive influence, parties, or pressure groups would almost certainly weaken liberal democracy.

Since representatives do more than express the general and particular wills of their constituents, it is important to examine who they are. In the United States and in Italy, the legal profession is a major source for candidates for the legislatures. The preponderance of legislators trained in the law found in these countries is sometimes explained partly on the grounds that it is rational to call upon jurists as legislators and partly because members of the bar lose little or nothing in their professional careers by taking a few years out for political work. Adlai Stevenson and Richard Nixon had this in common: each, after his defeat in a presidential election, was able to return to the bar with an enhanced position. Had they been physicians, architects, scholars (other than political scientists), military men, trade unionists, or almost anything else, they would probably have found their time off in politics a handicap rather than a help in their profession.

There is a further explanation for the large number of lawyers in Italian politics. There it is less the result of compatibility between the professions of law and politics than a reflection of the surfeit of lawyers. The law degree, which in the United States is one of the most prestigious and intellectually taxing of the graduate degrees, is in Italy perhaps the least demanding of the traditional degrees. The social significance of the Italian law degree thus is roughly equivalent to an American B.A. at the turn of the century, when the B.A. was an élite symbol, signifying little beyond an average mind, a good secondary education, and four years of leisure in which to enjoy life.

The Bundestag, in contrast to these lawyer-ridden legislatures, is administration-oriented. Doctor's degrees abound, and the largest professional group is made up of career civil servants on leave. Pressure groups, if they are well organized, are usually also well represented.[39] A recent study of Norwegian representatives by Henry Valen[40] shows a strong preference on the part of the voters of all five major parties for electing to the Storting representatives of organizations such as trade unions, farm groups, and religious groups.

The traditional peculiarity of the French parliament was the relatively high percentage of journalists and the large number of locally elected government officials, usually mayors, among its members. The Riksdag, the Storting, the Assemblée fédérale, and the Staaten Generaal also contain many persons with long experience in local government.[41]

Perhaps the most significant long-term trend in the quality of legislators is an increasing professionalism. The advent of strong parties, the use of proportional representation, and the increase in informal functional representation have all helped to decrease the turnover in parliament and to transform what was once an avocation for the wealthy and well-born or the young and the

[39] See Gerhard Loewenberg, *Parliament in the German Political System* (Ithaca, N.Y.: Cornell University Press, 1966), pp. 40–130.

[40] Reported in *News of Norway,* March 21, 1966, p. 43.

[41] "Some 50% [of the Riksdagsmän] have county council functions and about 70% serve on various posts in the local districts"—Andrén, *op. cit.,* p. 57. For Norway, see *News of Norway, loc. cit.;* for Switzerland, Hughes, *op. cit.,* pp. 52–53; for the Netherlands, Robert W. Morton, "Central Government Control of Municipalities in the Netherlands," *Western Political Quarterly,* XXX (1939), 64–70.

daring into a reasonably attractive and secure career.[42] Party politics is no place for dilettantes; party strength is built on professionalism. It is the party's job to see that the party regulars get elected to office, and if it is to be successful it must win elections not only for the label but for the inner group of professionals that controls the party.

A major effect of proportional representation is to increase the number of safe seats in parliament. Such seats offer better career opportunities and thereby encourage professionalism in politics. The trend toward informal functional representation has the same effect, as the pressure group prefers to be represented by an experienced member of parliament rather than by a freshman.

The practice of culminating a career initiated in local government with a seat in parliament, already noted as a pattern in many states of western Europe, is another indication of professionalism. The tendency toward professionalism is noted even in the United States, where the factors mentioned above are less important.[43] Only in large, short-term bodies like the Vermont legislature do dilettantes continue to flourish.

Ꝓarliamentary Organization

The organization of parliament has much to do with its operation and efficiency, and a preconditioning factor in organization is the size of the legislative chamber. The House of Commons and the Camera dei deputati have over 600 members each. The Bundestag, the House of Representatives, and the Assemblée

[42] Christopher Hughes (*The Parliament of Switzerland* [London: Cassel & Co., Ltd., 1962], pp. 53–54) estimates that about half the members of the Swiss parliament are professionals. Sir Edward Fellowe ("Changes in Parliamentary Life, 1918–1961," *Political Quarterly*, XXXVI [1965], 256–265) notes a trend toward increased professionalism in the House of Commons. Loewenberg (*op. cit.*) maintains that the Bundestag is controlled by the professional career politicians among its members.

[43] H. Douglas Price, unpublished manuscript, "The Congressional Career —Risks and Rewards."

nationale have between 400 and 500 members; the Senato has over 300. The Canadian lower house, the Sénat, the Andra Kammar, and the Chambre des représentants have from 200 to 300 members, while the Folketing, the Storting, the Förste Kammar, the Tweede Kamer, the Belgian Senate, the Conseil national, the Australian House of Representatives, and the Knesset each have over 100 members.[44] All of these bodies are too large for a fruitful give-and-take, for careful consideration and compromise.

The various bodies have sought to overcome this difficulty in divers ways, of which the most important is the standing committee, which has been defined as one that sits permanently. The normal committee system gives each committee competence over certain related subjects and requires all proposed legislation on those subjects to be submitted to the competent committee for scrutiny. Studying the bill and amending it as seems to them desirable, the committee reports on the bill to the full assembly, which normally accepts the recommendation of the committee.

One advantage of the committee system is that it makes it possible for all bills to be scrutinized by a small group of legislators who have the time and opportunity to become acquainted with them. Since committee members, by and large, may remain on the same committee if they so desire for their entire legislative career, they have the opportunity to gain experience and to become experts in the field of their committee's competence.[45] If they lack the ability and the inclination to become experts themselves, they can still be the mouthpiece of their party's policy on the matter at hand. And by their central position in the legislative process for the bills referred to their committee, they will

[44] For a detailed but legalistic account of the organization of the houses of parliament in Great Britain, France, Italy, Belgium, Spain, and Portugal, and a detailed description of their physical setting, see "A organização eo funcionamento do poder legislativo," *op. cit.*

[45] This tendency is further encouraged in the United States by the seniority system, based on length of service on the committee and not in Congress. For a discussion of the seniority system, see George Goodwin, Jr., "The Seniority System in Congress," *American Political Science Review,* LIII (1959), 412–436, and Emanuel J. Celler, "The Seniority Rule in Congress," *Western Political Quarterly,* XIV (1961), 160–167.

hear most of the arguments pro and contra expressed by the various groups that seek the bill's enactment or its interment.

The number of standing committees and the fields of their competence vary considerably from state to state. The competence, however, is often equivalent to that of a ministry. Thus there is often a special relationship between the senior members of a standing committee and the senior bureaucrats of a particular ministry. Under the Fourth Republic, France had a standing committee (1 of 19) devoted exclusively to alcohol;[46] the Assemblée nationale of the Fifth Republic, on the other hand, is limited by the constitution to 6 standing committees.

Unusual features of the standing committees in the various countries include the Swedish joint committees, the Italian "legislative" committees, and the special powers granted the Rules Committee of the United States House of Representatives. The two houses of the Swedish Riksdag have joint standing committees (*ständiga utskott*), with the result that bills go to committee only once and are reported out in identical form to both houses. The joint committee is an old Swedish tradition dating from the quadri-cameral period in Swedish parliamentary history, when joint committees were a virtual necessity. The Swedish system appears to have much to recommend it, but it has not been widely copied except in Norway, where the Odelsting and the Lagting form common committees (*Komiteer*). Somewhat similar systems are in effect, however, in Connecticut, Maine, and Massachusetts.[47]

The Italian standing committees (*commissioni permanenti*) may act in the normal way. But the Italian constitution permits the committees to which bills are referred to make final disposition of them, to act *in sede deliberante*. Certain types of bills, however, are not liable to this procedure. The exceptional matters include constitutional reform, ratification of treaties, budgets, delegation of legislative power to the executive, electoral law,

---

[46] See P. A. Bromhead, "Some Notes on the Standing Committees of the French National Assembly," *Political Studies,* V (1957), 140–157.

[47] See Duane Lockhart, *New England State Politics* (Princeton, N.J.: Princeton University Press, 1959), pp. 149, 283.

and in the chamber alone, taxes. The major weakness of this system is that since committee meetings are secret, laws can be passed without any public hearing and without the voters having any knowledge of how anyone voted. Under the Italian system, there is often sufficient party discipline for major legislation to be voted according to party instructions, but it would appear highly and dangerously undemocratic to pass any laws in secrecy. Deputies all over the world are tempted to succumb to pressure and to forget now and then to follow their own or their constituents' inclinations. In countries other than Italy they must do so more openly (if they do it at all) and take the consequences.[48]

The Rules Committee of the United States House of Representatives is a striking example of a committee that is given power over other committees. According to house procedure, a bill after committee deliberation cannot be reported back to the whole house without affirmative action on the part of the Rules Committee.[49] Even when they are deprived of the dangerous additional prerogatives of the Italian committees and the United States Rules Committee, however, the concentration of power in the hands of a few men has its inconvenient side. The *de facto* power that most committees may exercise by failing to report bills back to the legislature makes the committee a focus of attention for pressure groups, particularly in countries like the United States, where party discipline in voting is weak.[50] Since it is usually in committee that the bill takes its final form, pressure groups are always interested in bringing to bear what influence they can to see that as much good or as little harm as possible will be done their cause by committee amendments.

[48] For a reasoned attack on the system, see Luigi Einaudi, *Lo scrittoio del Presidente* (Turin: Giulio Einaudi, 1956), pp. 17–19.

[49] There are exceptions to the veto power of the Rules Committee. For detailed information, see James Robinson, *The House Rules Committee* (Indianapolis: The Bobbs-Merrill Co., Inc., 1963). For a case study, see H. Douglas Price, "Race, Religion, and the Rules Committee," in Alan Westin (ed.), *The Uses of Power* (New York: Harcourt, Brace & World, Inc., 1962), pp. 2–71.

[50] See, for instance, Berman, *op. cit.*, pp. 99–101.

The organization of committees is usually determined by the rules that parliament itself sets. In Sweden and France, however, these matters are not left to parliamentary discretion. In Sweden, the Riksdag Act (*Riksdagsordningen*) is one of the four principal documents that make up the Swedish constitution.[51] The French constitution (Arts. 40–43) sets the basic rules for parliamentary organization and procedure.

Standing committees with a specialized competence are the most common, but not the only method of dividing legislatures into smaller and more efficient deliberative units. The British tradition in the House of Commons has been to rely on five unspecialized committees and a committee for Scotland, the latter composed of the 71 Scottish members plus a dozen or so others.[52] The Scottish Committee receives the bills that concern Scotland specifically. Such bills are numerous because Scotland has its own educational, legal, and ecclesiastical institutions and procedures.[53] The other five committees, traditionally composed of a core of some 20 members and an additional group of around the same number expressly for the consideration of each single bill, are *de iure* competent to consider any bill. In practice they are nearly as specialized as committees in other countries. This is so for three reasons: (1) the five unspecialized standing committees no longer have a core membership; (2) there is now a tendency to assign bills dealing with similar matters to the same committte; and (3) in assigning members to a committee, the special competencies of members of parliament are taken into consideration. Thus, as Professor K. C. Wheare has suggested, the major difference between the normal and the British practice is that in the former the bills go to the experts, and in the latter the experts go to the bills.[54] For some time, parliament there has had special-

[51] See Andrén, *op. cit.*, pp. 13–14.

[52] J. H. Burns, "The Scottish Committee of the House of Commons," *Political Studies*, VIII (1960), 272–296.

[53] A similar Welsh committee has been established, but as there are no separate educational, ecclesiastical, and juridical systems in Wales, it has little to do.

[54] K. C. Wheare, *Government by Committee* (London: Oxford University Press, 1951), p. 135.

ized select committees (i.e., committees established for a single session of parliament). Some of these are important, for example, the committees on estimates, on public accounts, on selections, on nationalized industries, on standing orders, and on statutory instruments. In 1966, a further step toward specialist committees was made by the creation of two special standing committees on agriculture and on science and technology.

Another peculiarity of the British committee system is that bills go to committee after they have been approved in principle by the house in a second reading. This displacement of the committee phase to a later step in the formal legislative process inhibits the committee from effective control of general policy questions, and tends to restrict its attention to matters of detail.[55] The Danish practice is somewhat similar. Bills are normally sent to an ad hoc committee, rather than to one of the eight standing committees of the Folketing, which are primarily concerned with general policy questions.[56]

A peculiarity of the legislative process in Australia eliminates the committee stage in the iter of a bill.[57] The relatively small size of the Australian houses (124 and 60) makes it feasible to substitute the committee of the whole for standing committees.

At a time when the British are moving cautiously toward the system of specialized standing committees, the French are imposing the old British system on France. The 19 specialized standing committees of the Fourth Republic have been abolished, and the new parliament is limited by the constitution to 6 standing committees, which, again copying the British, are not specialized, and are too large to serve a useful purpose. The fact that the French constitution gives the government the right to disregard committee amendments and present government bills to parlia-

[55] See Richard Rose, *Politics in England* (Boston: Little, Brown & Co., 1964), p. 215; and Michael Ryle, "Committees in the House of Commons," *Political Quarterly*, XXXVI (1965), 295–308.

[56] Kenneth E. Miller, *Government and Politics in Denmark* (Boston: Houghton Mifflin Company, 1968), pp. 131–136.

[57] See G. S. Reid, "Australia's Commonwealth Parliament and the 'Westminster Model,'" *Journal of Commonwealth Political Studies*, II (1964), 89–101.

ment in their original form (Art. 41) must further discourage committee initiative and responsibility.

A former French system, that of the sections, is still in use in Belgium, Luxembourg, and the Netherlands. By this system, the assembly is divided by lot into three (Luxembourg) or five (Belgium and the Netherlands) divisions of approximately equal size in such a way that every member of the assembly is a member of one section. Its major advantage is to let three to five persons talk about the same thing at the same time and thereby elicit greater participation in parliamentary debate than is possible when all the representatives meet together. But the use of the sections is declining. A half century ago in Belgium there were more section meetings than standing committee meetings; now the ratio is about 100:1 in favor of the committees.[58] The Netherlands still makes use of sections for political matters on which many want to have their say, but here too the use of commissions is increasing.[59] Only in Luxembourg does the section system still flourish, but even in this last stronghold the standing committee is also used.[60]

The committee of the whole house is an Anglo-American device that seems to simplify the formalities and to speed up the work of an assembly by relaxing the rules. Such a committee offers no advantage in size, but it benefits from many of the other advantages of committee proceedings over those of a full, formally constituted parliament.

Another division of parliament that creates groups that may play a significant role in the legislative process is the division by party. The parliamentary groups are important formal divisions of the French, Italian, and German legislatures. In the Anglo-American world, they are equally important but they are not a part of the formal organization of parliament. In all liberal democracies these bodies play a key role in determining the

[58] Fusilier, *op. cit.*, p. 475.

[59] *Ibid.*, pp. 544–545; and E. Van Raalte, *The Parliament of the Netherlands* (London: Hansard Society, 1959), pp. 168–170.

[60] Fusilier, *op. cit.*, pp. 586–588.

policy of the party toward specific bills, and in most parliaments party discipline provides bloc voting.

The British habit of setting up informal committees composed of the members of parliament representing a given party, who are interested in a given field, creates a kind of in-service training program for the participants. These committees meet frequently to discuss policy and to listen to outside experts, who are invited to present their opinions and technical knowledge. By their activities, such committees create a reserve of experienced and trained MP's in the various fields, on which the party can draw for future ministers.

Where party cohesion is weak, subgroups within the parliamentary group meet and agree to vote together. This practice is particularly common in Italy and the United States.[61]

In those countries with relatively weak parliamentary standing committees and investigatory committees, there is often a tradition of executive appointment of expert committees. The British royal commissions are the example that first comes to mind. These are ad hoc bodies made up of highly respected experts and generalists, who study a given problem for months or years and prepare a report for the government. This report may be the basis for future legislation and/or policy changes.

The Swedish government makes much use of royal commissions both for the important matters dealt with by a British royal commission and for considerably more minor matters. In the latter case, the Swedish commissions may consist of a single commissioner. They are appointed by the king in council (that is, the cabinet), often on petition by the Riksdag, and are composed of parliamentarians and experts who can call in other expert testimony.[62]

---

[61] See, for example, Raphael Zariski, "Intra-party Conflict in a Dominant Party," *Journal of Politics*, XXVII (1965), 11–65; Alan Fiellin, "The Functions of Informal Groups in Legislative Institutions," *Journal of Politics*, XXIV (1962), 72–91; and David B. Truman, "The State Delegations and the Structure of Party Voting in the U.S. House of Representatives," *American Political Science Review*, L (1956), 1023–1046.

[62] Andrén, *op. cit.*, pp. 158–162.

Near-American equivalents to these commissions include the Warren Commission, and the two Hoover commissions on government reorganization. Such commissions are abnormal procedures for the American government, as the United States congress usually prefers to do its own investigating by calling in civil servants and outside experts to testify. Such investigations may be done by the regular standing committees or by special ad hoc committees. In spite of the fact that ad hoc investigating committees can frequently more than justify their existence by the legislation they eventually foster, they may be suspect in the public eye because of the great publicity they afford their chairmen and the misuse to which they have been put by a few publicity-seeking witchhunters.

It is the Swiss practice to appoint ad hoc expert committees to examine important bills before submission to parliament.[63] Many Italian ministries have permanent expert advisory committees that are normally consulted during the preparation of government bills falling within their competence. The German system is to present the bills for preliminary scrutiny to the Bundesrat, which has apposite standing committees composed of Länder civil servants.

Bi-cameralism, once a limitation of democratic law, is today— now that both houses are either democratically elected or responsible to a democratically elected political party—popular, effective, and reasonable only where there are significant differences in the type of membership and the functions of the two houses. Thus it serves little purpose in the 49 bi-cameral American states or in Italy, where the two houses are virtually replicas of each other. The prestige of the Senate in Canada[64] is low as a

[63] See Hughes, op. cit., pp. 106–108.

[64] The opening paragraph in the chapter on the Senate in the "classic" textbook on Canadian government reads as follows: "Canada is slowly developing some institutions of government, which if they cannot yet be placed in the vestigial class, are in danger of attaining that questionable distinction. The Senate . . . is all too clearly becoming undermined by forces which threaten to lead to eventual obscurity and obsolescence. . . .

"A very troublesome problem which is rarely absent from the mind of a Prime Minister is how to get rid of dead wood in his Cabinet, men . . . whose best days are over and who may or may not still have a modest con-

result of the poor quality of its members, the relatively unrepresentative nature of the selection procedure, and its limited and at the same time redundant powers. The same holds true in the long run for the French Sénat, although this body, which de Gaulle wished virtually to destroy, in 1969 won the probably temporary and unmerited affection of the majority of the French as a rallying point for anti-de-Gaullism. On the other hand, the United States Senate is a respected organ, and persuasive arguments can be made in favor of the House of Lords, the Erster Kamer, the Bundesrat, and the Conseil des états. Although copied after the United States Senate, the Australian Senate has aroused little enthusiasm.[65]

The prestige of the United States Senate is derived from the caliber of its members, which has been consistently superior to that of the congressmen, and from the important additional powers bestowed on it by the constitution in approving treaties and many presidential appointments.

The recent reforms of the House of Lords[66]—which include the creation of life peerages for persons other than the law lords, the (so far) modest use of this power to appoint life peers from the Commonwealth and the Nonconformist clergy, the payment of a *per diem* to members while attending sessions, and the right of hereditary peers to divest themselves of their rank and

---

tribution to make to public life. . . . The honest and fitting thing to do would be to give them a generous pension. . . . A worse plan, but one which has been quietly followed for years, is to place the Minister in the Senate pasture for the rest of his days"—R. MacGregor Dawson, *The Government of Canada* (3d ed., Toronto: University of Toronto Press, 1963), pp. 303, 311. See also R. A. MacKay, *The Unreformed Senate of Canada* (London: Oxford University Press, 1956); and Henry S. Albinski, "The Canadian Senate: Politics and the Constitution," *American Political Science Review,* LVII (1963), 378–391.

[65] See Anthony Fusaro, "The Australian Senate as a House of Review: Another Look," *Australian Journal of Politics and History,* XII (1966), 384–399; and R. H. C. Loof, "The Legislative Process in the Senate," *Public Administration* (Australia), XXIII (1964), 146–158.

[66] See, for instance, Vincent Weare, "The House of Lords, Prophecy and Fulfillment," *Parliamentary Affairs,* XVIII (1965), 422–433.

consequently to become eligible for election to the Commons—
have tended to reduce the class distinction between the houses.
They have also laid stress on the functional distinction between
a large, popularly elected house and a small appointive chamber,
where experts can debate policy and suggest technically appropriate amendments on a relatively nonpartisan basis.[67]

The motive for the creation of the Dutch Erste Kamer in
1813 was the traditional one espoused by conservatives: it was
advocated as a brake on any overhasty action by the Tweede
Kamer, to preserve the balance between the sovereign and the
people.[68] Until 1848, membership was for life by royal appointment; after this date, it was by indirect election by the provincial
councils. Peculiarities in the powers of the Erste Kamer include
the following: (1) It can initiate no legislation, (2) it has no
powers of amendment, and (3) it has an absolute veto over all
bills. It is thus not concerned with the technical details of
legislation but only with matters of broad policy, and supposedly
represents the sober second thought of the nation. During the
last century it has rejected about one bill a year;[69] in spite of
its distinctive powers, however, there is a movement afoot to
abolish it.

The German Bundesrat is an institution compatible with the
system of division of powers practiced in the German and
Swiss federations. In this system a large part of the legislative
power is in the hands of the federal unit, while most of the
administrative power is exercised at the Länder level.[70] The

[67] Other recent reforms are the seating of peeresses in their own right and
the seating of all the Scottish peers, instead of, as formerly, merely a representation of 16 Scottish peers chosen by and from among themselves. These
changes appear of little importance except as indicative of a sort of democratic egalitarianism that equates females and Scots with the English male.
The Wilson government proposed further changes in 1967, but does not seem
ready to pass further legislation before calling new elections.

[68] Van Raalte, *op. cit.*, p. 58.

[69] *Ibid.*, p. 61.

[70] In a four-year period the federal government enacted 483 laws, while
in a two-year period the Rheinland-Palatinate and Hessen enacted 30 and
22 respectively. See Peter H. Merkl, "Legislative Federalism in West Germany," *American Political Science Review*, LIII (1950), 732–741.

Bundesrat, which represents the Länder and whose members are appointed by the Länder executives, represents the prejudices and expertise of the formidable, prestigious German bureaucracy. The fact that on the one hand the federal government is not responsible to the Bundesrat, and that on the other the Bundesrat has an absolute veto over most legislation, makes it a most distinctive body. There is considerable difference of opinion over the amount of actual power wielded by the Bundesrat, but no one claims that it is a pale and wan replica of the Bundestag.[71]

The parliaments of Norway and Iceland—the Storting and the Althing—offer examples of a hybrid form between uni- and bi-cameralism, in which a single elected house coopts a minority of its members to form a second house, which in some ways constitutes a committee of parliament rather than a second chamber. The Norwegian name of this coopted chamber is the Lagting, and when the Lagting sits separately, the remaining members of the Storting (Norwegian for "the big assembly") make up the Odelsting.

The peculiar way in which the Storting divides itself into two "chambers" (for specific purposes only) is not of Nordic origin. More than a hundred years before the Norwegians put their system into practice, it received the blessing of John Adams, who wrote,

> Let the representative assembly then elect by ballot, from among themselves or their constituents or both, a distinct assembly which, for the sake of perspicuity, we will call a council. It may consist of any number you please, say twenty or thirty, and should have a free and independent exercise of its judgment and consequently a negative voice in the legislature.[72]

---

[71] See, for example, Edward L. Pinney, *Federalism, Bureaucracy, and Party Politics in the West German Bundesrat* (Chapel Hill, N.C.: University of North Carolina Press, 1963); Karlheinz Neunreither, "Politics and Bureaucracy in the West German Bundesrat," *American Political Science Review*, LIII (1959), 713–731; and Loewenberg, *Parliament in the German Political System*.

[72] Adams, *op. cit.*, p. 88.

Adams, as well as the Norwegians, was probably inspired by a similar institution that operated in the Dutch Batavian Republic.

The Norwegian constitution, Article 41, states: "The people shall exercise the legislative power through the Storting, which consists of two divisions, the Lagting and the Odelsting." Article 75 enumerates "the duties and prerogatives of the Storting," among which are (a) to enact and repeal laws, (b) to negotiate loans, and (c) to control the finances of the kingdom.

The framers of the constitution refrained from putting down in writing how these different duties were to be carried out in the Storting, and left it to this body to decide its own internal division of labor. This was a matter of great concern in the first decades after 1814. By 1830, however, it had been largely settled in the present form. In practice, the two divisions are used only for the enactment and repeal of *lover* (laws in the restricted sense of acts that affect or regulate the rights and duties of citizens and their relations with the state). The remaining laws—called *resolusjoner* and including such heterogeneous matters as budgets, approval of treaties, granting citizenship, and constitutional amendments—are handled by the Storting as a unit.[73]

The wisdom of the division into Odelsting and Lagting has many times been questioned. Several proposals to make the Lagting into a true second chamber were put forward in 1821 and 1880. Proposals to do away with it altogether were made in 1927 by the Labor Party, which would like to see "laws" enacted by the procedure of two readings in the Storting. But a government study in 1936 [74] advised against change; it felt that greater guarantees for good legislation were secured through the existing system. The Ministry of Justice suggested that if the divisions were to be abolished, it would be advisable to introduce popular referenda as part of the lawmaking procedure.

Proposals to do away with the divisions were again put forward in 1935, 1951, and 1954, the last two being dismissed without

[73] Fusilier, *op. cit.,* pp. 262–264.

[74] *St. melding,* No. 26, 1936: *Om Stortingets Lovbehandling.*

debate. The political parties have in reality made the two chambers copies of each other. The function of the Lagting today appears to be only that of an overseer or reviser of technical details, but as the Lagting members are not distinguished from their colleagues in the Odelsting by either experience or legal training, this is a meager basis on which to maintain the Lagting —particularly since the scrutiny to which legislative proposals are subject in the ministries and committees appears to be a sufficient guarantee against legislative oversight.[75] That nothing has been done to eliminate the "constitutional anachronism" of these divisions may be due to the fact that the Lagting is a part of the Impeachment Court, a highly respected institution in Norway because in 1882 it was instrumental in establishing the practice of parliamentarianism.

Today, the importance of the Storting as a whole completely overshadows that of its divisions. This is because all financial matters, foreign policy matters, concessions, interpellations, and questions are the business of the Storting as a body. The Lagting is not an independent center of power: it is in the Storting that the political disagreements between cabinet and parliament are settled.

Luxembourg operates another type of pseudo bi-cameralism in which the chief administrative organ of the state, the Conseil d'état, acts as the pseudo second chamber. All bills must be presented to the Conseil d'état for its opinion before the final vote. The normal procedure is to seek the opinion of the Conseil before the bills are presented to parliament; in this case, any bill that is amended in parliament is resubmitted to the Conseil before the final vote. If the Conseil does not approve the bill in its final form, it has a three-month suspensive veto, after which the bill must start over at the beginning of the normal parliamentary procedure for a new bill, except that this time the bill becomes law if passed by parliament even without the approval of the Conseil.[76]

[75] Finn Hiorthøy, "Lagtingets stilling etter norsk forfatning," *Festskrift til Professor Dr. Juris Poul Andersen* (Copenhagen: Danmarks Juristforbund, 1958), pp. 183–198.

[76] Fusilier, *op. cit.*, pp. 581–586.

Another of the traditional conceptual dichotomies found in many texts on comparative political institutions is that of parliamentary and presidential systems.

By separating the policy-proposing function (assigned to the cabinet) from the policy-approving function (reserved to parliament), the parliamentary system, which at first sight appears to concentrate political authority in the same hands, actually establishes an effective separation of function within a single coordinated unit. In this way, the few in the cabinet prepare and propose, and the more in parliament dispose after consideration of the wishes and the welfare of the community. When policy must be implemented by legislation the pattern is clear, in that the modifications and initiation of policy by parliament can be observed in the formal lawmaking procedure. When policy is implemented by executive order, the influence of parliament is formally recorded in the exercise of its powers of investigating legislative activity and questioning it. Only rarely has it a *de iure* veto over administrative acts. Normally its weapon is publicity, and its sanction the threat and danger of public disapproval.

In orthodox parliamentary systems, a mutual check is exercised by cabinet and parliament in that parliament may overthrow the cabinet by a vote of no confidence, and the cabinet can ask the titular head of state to dissolve parliament. In Canada and Great Britain, only the lower house has the power to overthrow the government and is liable to dissolution. In Australia, although both houses may be dissolved, a vote against the government in the Senate is not likely to cause resignation of the government.[77] The Norwegian system includes the vote of confidence but does not allow dissolution. The Swedish and Netherlands systems, on the other hand, permit dissolution and do not include a formal requirement that the cabinet resign when it fails to retain the confidence of parliament. These variants, however, are of little importance, as the convention in these three exemplary democracies is for effective cooperation

[77] Crisp, *op. cit.*, p. 181.

between these branches of government. The German requirement of a so-called constructive vote of no confidence causes more legitimate concern because, unless tempered by a convention of cooperation that may develop through the years, it may lead to the elimination of effective liberal democracy in Germany. The constructive vote of no confidence is actually a majority vote of confidence in some single person other than the chancellor. This system permits a chancellor to remain in office without the confidence of parliament so long as parliament does not agree on a successor. As Professor Herz has observed, "At present a parliamentary system can hardly be said to exist. . . . Under these conditions Cabinet responsibility is hardly a problem, but responsible government in the British sense is." [78]

The presidential system, which at first sight would appear to offer a greater safeguard against an undemocratically used concentration of power in a single government organ, has produced far inferior results in practice. This system has worked best in the United States, where neither organ has consistently effective control over the other. France permits dissolution of the Assemblée nationale by the president but provides no way to remove the president short of impeachment. Thus power there is effectively concentrated in the hands of the president. The Assemblée does have the right to vote no confidence in the premier, but this power is carefully circumscribed in the constitution and the one time such a vote was passed against Premier Georges Pompidou, the result was the dissolution of the Assemblée by the president and the continuation of Pompidou in office.

The history of South America offers countless other examples of the failure of presidential systems, because of the failure to stem the dictatorial propensities of the president. The examples of failure through legislative interference with the executive are less numerous but not unknown, at least in Chile.[79]

[78] John H. Herz, in Gwendolyn Carter and John Herz, *The Major Foreign Powers* (4th ed.; New York: Harcourt, Brace, 1962), p. 434.

[79] See, for example, Luis Galdames, *Estudio de la historia de Chile* (8th ed., Santiago: Editorial Nascimento, 1938), ch. XIX.

As is so often the case, however, when theorists attempt to clarify political thinking by comparing and drawing distinctions, there is danger that the very distinctions become fetishes. We have already seen this in the dichotomy of policy and administration and in the doctrine of the separation of powers. Sir Denis Brogan has warned us of a similar danger in distinguishing between presidential and parliamentary government. In writing of the many mixed systems, primarily parliamentary (*de iure*), and primarily presidential (*de facto*), in former British Africa, Sir Denis adds: "It can be said without producing indignant denial or effective refutation . . . that England herself is moving towards a presidential system of government with the Prime Minister as the equivalent of the President." [80]

Legislative-executive relations are handled in a different fashion in Switzerland. By convention, the executive is supreme and parliament has abdicated the right to initiate legislation; although it elects the seven-man executive every four years, it has never had the right to force executive resignations. It is submitted that the Swiss system would constitute a viable democratic process only in a country with no serious opposition. Swiss reliance on a concurrent majority government representing seven eighths of the voters creates a form of government quite different from the British model. It is true that the Swiss have not always been so tolerant. After the war of the Sonderbund, Roman Catholic opposition was given short shrift by the dominant Radicals, but later in the century they adopted a policy of "If you can't beat 'em, join 'em," and accepted in the government first Catholics, later Farmers, and then Socialists. By this device, the Swiss Radicals have established a record of 120 consecutive years in power. By eliminating effective opposition, the Swiss governments have been able to concentrate on matters of administrative rather than political moment and have reduced significantly the kind of unproductive political jockeying that has seriously weakened the liberal democratic governments in France and Italy.

[80] Sir Denis Brogan, "The Possibilities of the Presidential System in Africa," in Sir Alan Burns (ed.), *Parliament as an Export* (London: Allen and Unwin, Ltd., 1966), pp. 190–207 at 191.

Parliamentary Procedures

Perhaps the surest rule-of-thumb indication of how far a given parliamentary system has evolved from the classical legislative theory of liberal democracy is seen in the quality of restrictions placed on the initiation of bills by the member of parliament. According to the classical theory, it is the individual deputy who is expected to initiate legislation. Such was in fact the practice at one time. It is still common in the United States and in Italy. In other liberal democracies the right of the individual member to initiate legislation is severely limited by law or convention, and the executive has become the normal source for legislative policy. Such limitations are in effect in Great Britain, France, Israel, Switzerland, Sweden, Germany, and Norway.

The British MP must ballot (that is, draw lots) for the privilege of introducing a single bill annually; the bill may appropriate or spend no money, and has no chance of enactment without at least the benevolent neutrality of the government. Most private member bills deal with matters on which the government takes no stand (for example, blue laws, SPCA laws, laws dealing with sexual deviates).[81] The French procedures under the Fifth Republic are copied after those of the House of Commons without, however, limiting the number of bills that each deputy may present (Art. 40). The Israeli practice is similar to that of Great Britain and France, although it is less crystallized in conventions than the British practice and lacks the legally enforceable constitutional quality of the French provision.

Members of the Swiss parliament refrain from introducing any bills, but they do present postulats and motions to the Federal Council (the executive power) for its consideration. A *postu-*

---

[81] See Michael Ryle, "Private Members' Bills," *Political Quarterly,* XXXVII (1966), 385–393; Ernest Davies, "The Role of Private Members' Bills," *Political Quarterly,* XXVIII (1957), 32–39; and Rupert Speir, "The Promotion of a Private Member's Bill," *Parliamentary Affairs,* XII (1958–59), 85–88.

lat is a request that some action be taken on a specific matter and is sent to the Council on approval by one house of parliament; a *motion* demands that action be taken on the matter, and must be approved by both houses before submission. Neither is draft legislation, but either may be a request for it.[82] The Council is free to act on the suggestions or not as it wishes.

The Swedish riksdagman may submit a motion to the house of which he is a member. This term applies to amendments to government bills (*propositioner*), to draft legislation, and to requests for consideration of specific matters on the part of the government. It is "extremely rare" that *motioner* are in the form of draft legislation. When they are, it is likely that they concern issues on which the parties dare not take a stand.[83]

The German requirement that 15 members must sign a bill before presentation means in effect that parties rather than individual members have the right of legislative initiative. In Norway, private member bills "are referred to the appropriate administrative departments for official consideration before being sent to the appropriate parliamentary committee. The practical effect of this policy has been to give the departments—that is to say, the Cabinet—control over most of the bills introduced in the Storting." [84]

The restrictions placed on private member bills and the insistence on party discipline do not mean that the independent member is helpless or impotent even in the countries where these practices pertain. If this were so, no pressure group would bother to have its man in parliament. The British private member, it is said, has a lot of influence if he has the ear and respect of his colleagues.[85]

Another function of the private member is to popularize in the country the policy of his party. This task is performed not only by publicizing and supporting that policy but by sanding off the rough spots particularly disagreeable to the part of the

[82] See Hughes, *op. cit.*, pp. 120–127.

[83] See Andrén, *op. cit.*, pp. 78–81; and Elis Håstad, *The Parliament of Sweden* (London: Hansard Society, 1957), pp. 97–102.

[84] Storing, *op. cit.*, p. 86.

[85] See Rose, *op. cit.*, pp. 212–215.

public he represents, or convincing the party leaders to do so. A private member may also, with a little brains, luck, and effort, become an expert in certain aspects of government and attain a position of prominence, prestige, and power that the government will not care to trifle with. This is certainly true for many of the senior members of the congressional and senatorial standing committees in the United States. The same can be said for the Scandinavian countries.

Particularly, but by no means exclusively, in the Anglo-American world, members of parliament are concerned with aiding their constitutents. One's representative is often the person to whom grievances against any government action are directed. The importance attached to this function in certain parliamentary states is attested to by the fact that when the New Zealand and British parliaments enacted legislation establishing an ombudsman, they forbade him to accept complaints directly from the public, empowering him to investigate only those complaints referred to him by members of parliament.

Various voting procedures are used in parliament, the most common being a showing of hands or a rising vote. Only the Anglo-Americans seem to have confidence in the viva voce vote. Perhaps only they have sufficiently inbred in them a dislike of shouting that makes the relative volume of the Ayes and Nays represent with reasonable accuracy the number of persons voting, rather than the sum of the passions generated by each side.

The British, the Germans, and the Italians have divisions, but they have little in common. In the British division, which is the method used for all important votes in that country, the members congregate in the house and, depending on whether their vote is Yes or No, file out of the apposite door, where tellers count the bodies and party whips spy out the absent.[86] The Germans divide by leaving the hall by any convenient exit and then

[86] One British critic says of this quaint British tradition: "As things are now, it would really be simpler and more economical to keep a flock of tame sheep and from time to time draw them through the division lobbies in the appropriate numbers . . ."—Christopher Hollis, *Can Parliament Survive?* (London: Hollis & Carter, Ltd., 1949), pp. 64–65.

returning through one of three doors, signifying by their choice
of door a Yes, No, or Abstaining vote. The Italians divide by
huddling in various corners of the assembly hall. They use this
method seldom, however, as it does not give substantially more
accurate results than the simple standing vote.

For situations that in Great Britain call for a division, most
other parliaments resort to a roll-call vote. This is a time-
consuming procedure, in which each member is called on in
turn to cast his vote orally. Legislators dislike it not only for
the time it wastes but because it publicizes each man's voting
record. The Italian, Netherlands, and Belgian roll calls all differ
from the American one in that the member whose name is
called first is chosen by lot and the call continues in alphabetical
order through Z back to A. The American method favors those
with names near the top of the alphabet because they are free
to leave as soon as their name is called, and it favors those
whose names are at the end of the alphabet in that they do not
need to commit themselves until they have learned how most
of the others have voted.

Alone of the major liberal democracies, Italy has retained
the policy of secret voting. This method appears highly undemocratic because it denies the electorate the right to know
how their representatives voted. It is defended on the grounds
that it permits the representatives to vote according to their
conscience without regard for the pressures of political parties or
vested interests. Actually, the system serves little useful purpose
because of the particular procedure used. The representatives
are each given a black and a white ball, and black and white
urns are placed before the presiding officer. As his name is called,
each representative approaches the urns and places one ball in
each. He who places the white ball in the white urn and the
black ball in the black one has cast an affirmative vote; he who
crosses the colors, a negative vote. In this way, it is easy for
members of parliament to see how a representive votes and the
only group kept in the dark is the electorate. The representative is no more able to fool the party hierarchy or the vested
interests under this system than under the system of an open
roll call, but the general public remains uninformed.

The contribution of modern science to parliamentary voting has been electric voting. Given the American passion for technology, it is natural that this system started in the United States, where reformers (e.g., Robert La Follette Sr.) and bosses (e.g., Huey Long) were quick to see its advantages. Under this system, a voter has buttons on his desk that connect to a conspicuously situated board. When the presiding officer calls for a vote he pulls a switch connecting the representatives' desks with the board, and the representatives have a few minutes to play with their buttons and to observe on the board how their colleagues are voting. When the time is up, the presiding officer disconnects the desks from the board and a photograph is taken of the board, thus recording the vote of each member. This system is fairly common in the United States, particularly among the larger lower houses. It has been exported to the French Assemblée nationale and to both branches of the Swedish Riksdag.

The traditional democratic procedure was that parliament should propose, perhaps as in Great Britain through petition, and that the executive might assent or reject. The modern procedure is rather the other way; it is usually the executive that proposes and it is parliament that exercises a veto, one however that may be used as sparingly as the old-fashioned executive veto.

The term "legislative veto" has both a restrictive and an extended meaning. In its more common and restrictive sense, it refers to the power of the legislature to abrogate administrative acts or to render them ineffective *ab initio*. Examples are the power of the British parliament over statutory instruments and that of the United States Congress over presidential reorganization of executive departments. A less savory device, the committee veto, by which a congressional committee can veto a specific administrative act (e.g., a real estate purchase) seems to be cropping up in the United States.[87]

In its broader sense, the term "legislative veto" may refer to the basic control parliament has over government policy. If the cabinet and the government constitute the first house in the

[87] See, for instance, Joseph P. Harris, *Congressional Control of Administration* (Garden City, N.Y.: Doubleday & Co., Inc., 1964), ch. 8.

modern legislative process, parliament still has the prerogatives
of a second house through the power of veto, and the individual
members of parliament may still have a lot to say about policy
in the fields of their competence, for only a foolhardy executive
would fail to take seriously into consideration the opinions and
desires of the men who are in the closest contact with the voters.

Furthermore, members of parliament on occasion are the
experts on the matter at hand, and their opinions merit careful
attention. This expertise may come from their extra-parliamentary careers or from their long association with a certain
sector of government through parliamentary specialization. As
mentioned earlier, pressure groups see to it that they have, if
not a representative, at least a friend in parliament to give
them inside information on legislation that concerns them.
Many legislators are altruistic and human enough to have pet
bills on which they are willing to spend a deal of effort, time,
and influence (for example, Senator Norris's Lame Duck Amendment and uni-cameral legislature for Nebraska).

In the United States and Scandinavia, where high-ranking
committee members may remain on the same committee for
their entire political life (this happens in the United States
because of the seniority system and in Scandinavia because
proportional representation virtually assures the reelection of
key men), considerable expertise in a field of legislation and
a good deal of political power may be found in the same person.

The party committees in the British parliament are primarily
in-service seminars for future ministers. An ambitious backbencher picks his field of specialization, and his advancement
depends in good measure on his ability to advise on policy.

In most parliamentary democracies the legislative veto is
used sparingly, but the ability and willingness of parliament to
scrutinize and publicize proposed legislation not to its liking
may cause the executive to give considerable weight to the
opinions of parliament. Italy is the parliamentary democracy
where the legislative veto is most used. This occurs because
party discipline in that country is too weak to guarantee a favorable vote on government bills.

In presidential systems the legislative veto is more common

and more out in the open, as Presidents Johnson and Frei have reason to know.

The private bill is primarily an Anglo-American device.[88] For continental jurists, law must be general and abstract; a private bill is specific and concrete—therefore it is not a law and cannot be enacted by parliament. The private bill, however, is quite a different animal on the two sides of the Atlantic. The British use the term for legislation dealing with a particular locality, such as, for instance, the Manchester Ship Canal Bill. Such bills exist on the European continent but are considered public.

A private bill in the United States is private in two senses. It concerns not more than a few specific persons, and not more than a few members of the legislature are concerned with it. Its purpose is the redress of some claimed injustice that one or more, but not many, individuals have suffered. These bills fall into three principal categories: bills granting relief for property damage or personal injury resulting from government action; immigration or naturalization bills; and private land bills. The American private bill thus is *sui generis* and permits the use of the legislative process for the redress of individual wrongs.[89]

The quantity and complexity of modern legislation is such that parliament is quite unable to perform the legislative function singlehanded. The delegation of legislative power to the executive is a frequently used method of relieving the strain on the legislature. There has been a deal of strife over just what is

[88] The private bill is also found in Chile. See Federico G. Gil, *The Political System of Chile* (Boston: Houghton Mifflin Company, 1966).

[89] Legislative justice, however, is not an American innovation. For some time the British parliament had regularly passed private acts affording equitable relief against fraud, duress, and breach of trust; such practice went out of use toward the end of the seventeenth century. Similarly, legislative criminal justice—such as acts of attainder and of pains and penalties—came to be regarded as vicious and obsolete in the eighteenth century. (See Roscoe Pound, *Administrative Law* [Pittsburgh, Pa.: University of Pittsburgh Press, 1942], p. 92.) In the United States, legislative criminal justice is prohibited by the federal constitution.

involved in the process of such delegation. The Lockeian theory of agency would ban it altogether[90] on the analogy of the British law of agency, which forbids the agent to redelegate power delegated by the principal.[91] A proposition that reaches the opposite conclusion is that since all volitional acts are acts of will, there is no difference in quality between an act that legislates and an act that delegates legislative power in that they are both expressions of parliament's will.[92]

Perhaps a more realistic approach views laws as of two types, (1) those that delimit interests, and (2) those that empower others to delimit interests.[93] The first type is preferred in relatively stable and static societies, the second in more dynamic periods of history. This distinction is related to the one that Professor McIlwain makes between *iurisdictio* and *gubernaculum*,[94] or that of Jouvenel between *rex* and *dux*.[95]

---

[90] *An Essay Concerning the True Original, Extent and End of Civil Government* (London, 1690), para. 141.

[91] Hence the transfer to constitutional law of the maxim from commercial law, *delegatus non potest delegari*.

[92] See, for example, Chief Justice White in *Clark Distilling Co.* v. *Western Maryland Railroad*, 242 U.S. 311 (1917) at 326; *Waterside Workers' Federation of Australia* v. *T. W. Alexander, Ltd.*, 52 *Commonwealth Law Reports* 434 (1919) at 463–464; and Piero Calamandrei, *Studi sul processo civile* (6 vols., Padua: CEDAM, 1934), Vol. III, pp. 153. A general discussion of this question and a presentation of the reasoning of these jurists is reported in John Clarke Adams, "Il controllo delle leggi costituzionali sulla delegazione del potere legislative," *Rivista di diritto pubblico*, XXXIX (1947), 26–33.

[93] See Francesco Carnelutti, *Sistemaadi diritto processuale civile* (6 vols., Padua: CEDAM, 1936), Vol. I, pp. 47–48, and John Clarke Adams, "Some Remarks on Carnelutti's System of Jurisprudence," *Ethics*, L (1939), 84–95. See also Wesley Newcomb Hohfeld, *Fundamental Jural Relations* (New Haven, Conn.: Yale University Press, 1923); L. L. Jaffe, "An Essay on Delegation of Legislative Power," *Columbia Law Review*, XLVII (1947), 359–376, 561–593; and H. L. A. Hart, *The Concept of Law* (Oxford: Clarendon Press, 1961), ch. 5. Professor Hart uses the terms "primary" and "secondary law."

[94] See Chapter 1 above. *Iurisdictio* is the law that delimits interests; *gubernaculum* the delegated power.

[95] Édouard Bertrand de Jouvenel des Ursins, *De la souveraineté* (Paris: Librairie de Medicis, 1955), pp. 34–35. *Rex* is the king under the law, *dux* is the leader who makes the law.

Modern parliaments have gone about divesting themselves of oppressive legislative power in various ways. In Norway and Holland, the custom is to delegate vast legislative power openly to the executive. The Italian constitution (Art. 76) authorizes parliament to delegate legislative powers to the government to fill in the detailed provisions of basic legislation, the general purport of which is stated in parliament's act of delegation. Such acts of executive legislation are known as *decreti legislativi*.

The widest use of this practice is found in France, where parliament on two occasions has turned over its powers to President de Gaulle with respect to a vast and vaguely defined subject matter for a period of months (Constitution, Art. 38). On February 2, 1960, the Assemblée and on the following day the Sénat conferred full legislative power on the government for a period of twelve months concerning "all measures necessary to maintain order, safeguard the state and the constitution, and to pacify and administer Algeria." In the spring of 1967, powers over general economic matters were delegated to the government for a period of six months. The acts that the government promulgates under such powers are called *ordinances;* they are presented to parliament for approval after the delegation of power has expired.

In Great Britain, provision is made for legislative assent to regulations issued under delegated authority. Such regulations are called statutory instruments and normally must be "laid before Parliament" for forty days prior to taking effect. Parliament's silence for this period is construed as assent.[96] The Americans have been guilty of a lot of pedantic hypocrisy on the subject of delegated legislative power but their common sense has seldom let it interfere with effective delegation, whether the subject matter was local home rule options, American Medical Association and American Bar Association control over professional qualifications, liquor laws, or the regulatory power of the independent regulatory commissions.[97]

[96] See J. F. Garner, *Administrative Law* (2d ed., London: Butterworth & Co., Ltd., 1967), pp. 67–68, for exceptions and further elucidation.

[97] See Mr. Justice Cardozo's delimitation of constitutional delegation of legislative power in *Panama Refining Co.* v. *Ryan,* 293 U.S. 388 (1935).

Sweden appears to be the exception to the tendency to delegate legislative power. There, either in deference to tradition or in order to avoid the violation of the shibboleth against such delegation, proposed legislation is drafted in detail before submission to the Riksdag.

Europeans in general use the term "delegated legislative power" in a restrictive sense. If the act of the administration is called a regulation, there is deemed to be no delegation of legislative power. As the line between law and regulation is a tenuous one, the actual powers of government to establish general and prospective norms through the regulatory power have no clear-cut limits. It is the custom in many European states for parliament to enact skeletal legislation and for the details to be supplied by the administration. This system is particularly appropriate in France, as the courts offer no protection against unconstitutional laws, while an administrative regulation may be and frequently is annulled by the Conseil d'état if it is in *excès de pouvoir* (that is, *ultra vires*).

When a state institutes a system of initiative and referendum, it would appear to diminish the political importance of parliament in the legislative process. Switzerland is the nation with the longest history of initiative and referendum and there the technical, nonpolitical aspects of parliament are apparent. De Gaulle's use of the plebiscite has reduced still further the prestige of the Assemblée nationale. When the Danes changed from bi-cameralism to uni-cameralism in 1953, they instituted a referendum that might be called by 30 per cent of the members of the Folketing, their remaining legislative body. The Danish convention by which legislation is normally passed by near consensus precludes frequent resort to this procedure. The first use of this referendum occurred in 1963, when the conservative forces succeeded in invalidating four socialist-inspired land laws by this method.[98] In 1969, a government proposal for adolescent suffrage for eighteen-year-olds was defeated in a referendum. The Italian parliament has been unwilling over a twenty-year

[98] See Miller, *op. cit.*, p. 138.

period to enact implementing legislation for the system of initiative and referendum outlined in its constitution. If ever the Italians have the opportunity to initiate and enact legislation without involving parliament, the latter will have lost a substantial amount of its power. It is expected, however, that legislation implementing initiative and referendum will be enacted in early 1970, as the Christian Democrats hope to rescind in this manner a mild divorce law for which they fear they will be unable to prevent parliamentary approval.

Norway and Australia, like Sweden, use a consultative referendum on occasion. The Swedish Riksdag has felt strong enough to override the will of the people as expressed in a consultative referendum: the people voted by a small majority to retain left-side driving, but parliament overruled them as the result of expert opinion which suggested that the Swedish practice caused many accidents when drivers crossed the borders separating Sweden from Norway and Denmark, where right-hand driving is the rule.

A traditional practice that tends today to create serious delays in the legislative process stems from the doctrine that bills not finally enacted before the expiration of a parliamentary mandate are to be reconsidered by the newly elected body. The whole procedure must be gone through again from the very beginning. The tradition is an anachronism predating liberal democratic government and is based on a powerful and active royal prerogative that could and did send parliament packing whenever the monarch saw fit to use it. It is strong in Great Britain, where it has a long history, and in Germany, where it has become a fixed principle of constitutional doctrine. It is still the practice in Italy, although there is considerable feeling in that country that it bears a significant share of the blame for the inability of the Italian parliament to enact many of the major reforms (such as revision of the law codes and reorganization of the public administration) for which republican Italy has been waiting for over a quarter of a century.

The tendency in liberal democracies today is to attenuate the effects of this doctrine of parliamentary discontinuity or to discard it completely. As is often the case in matters governmental,

however, an outmoded British tradition is more burdensome on
the rest of the world than on Britain itself. The House of Commons no longer follows its own tradition with respect to private
bills and does not always follow it with respect to public bills,
while the Germans, Italians, Australians, and Americans still conform to the former British practice. Other liberal democracies,
including Belgium, Israel, and the France of at least the Third
and Fourth Republics, follow a doctrine of parliamentary continuity.[99]

Cultural Influences

The success with which a government functions and the actual
procedures it follows depend in good part on the culture of the
social system in which it operates.[100] The same can be said for
the legislative process, which is a single aspect of the process
of government. Let us examine a few of the beliefs and behavior
patterns that appear significant in conditioning the legislative
process.

A culture that is dominated by conservative thought and that
has an aversion to sudden or drastic change prefers an ineffective
parliament. If the conservatives happen also to be devotees of
laissez-faire economics, their aversion to precipitous government
action is considerably reinforced. Many of the devices discussed
in Chapter III were conservative stratagems for debilitating the
radical or reformist energies of parliaments. The increasingly
democratic political structure of the West has eliminated a number of these stratagems, but the basic conservative bias still stands.
Thus the Republican Party, dominant in the United States for
most of a hundred years, is wedded to the principle that—with

[99] See Franco Bassanini, "Gli effetti della fine della legislatura sui procedi-
menti legislativi pendenti," *Rivista trimestrale di diritto pubblico,* XVIII
(1968), 721–804, 1186–1315.

[100] For a general discussion, see Gabriel A. Almond and G. Bingham
Powell, Jr., *Comparative Politics: A Developmental Approach* (Boston: Little,
Brown & Co., 1966), especially chs. II, IX, X.

a few exceptions such as tariffs—the least government is the best government. It has therefore exerted considerable ingenuity in developing a legislative process in America with bottlenecks controlled by Republicans (for example, the Speaker, the Rules Committee) better suited to the negative role of blocking legislation than formulating and executing policy changes.[101] The French Radical Party (Parti républicain radical et Radical socialiste), which represented the lay bourgeoisie of the French provinces, combined a love of individual freedom and a distrust of government interference with a passion to be in the government coalition in order to negate or at least mitigate its influence on the party's clientele.[102] The policies of these two parties have perhaps something to do with slowing the evolution of the legislative process in the United States and France.

Another significant distinction in the operation of legislatures lies in the relative importance the culture attaches to (1) thinking clearly, and (2) getting things done. French and Italian culture place a high priority on the former; the British and Dutch on the latter.[103]

The different emphasis these cultures place on individualistic speculative thought and cooperative action is reflected in the instability of the former governments and the relative stability of the latter. In seeking to explain the stability of the Netherlands governments, in spite of the five-party system in effect there and the necessity of forming governments out of coalitions of ideologically opposed political groups, Van Raalte says: "Political conditions in the Netherlands are such that people shrink from the necessity of forming a new cabinet." [104] If the French and Italians could only be convinced or conditioned to shrink under

[101] See E. E. Schattschneider, "United States: The Functional Approach to Party Government," in Sigmund Neuman (ed.), *Approaches to Comparative Politics* (Chicago: University of Chicago Press, 1956), pp. 194–215.

[102] See Francis De Tarr, *The French Radical Party in the Fourth Republic* (New York: Oxford University Press, 1961).

[103] For a brilliant analysis and contrast of British and French cultures, see Salvador de Madariaga, *Englishmen, Frenchmen, Spaniards* (London: Oxford University Press, 1928).

[104] Van Raalte, *op. cit.*, p. 32.

such circumstances, the prognosis for the successful continuance of liberal democracy in those countries would be significantly more hopeful. Frenchmen and Italians, however, can be strongly attached to *La France* and *L'Italia* respectively without having the slightest respect for the state or the government. In those cultures, patriotism attaches to an idea—the culture itself—rather than to an institution.

The serious lack of political consensus and the consequent distrust of the state found in France and Italy constitute a grave deterrent to the establishment of a viable and permanent liberal democracy in those countries and undermine the effective operation of parliament there. No state is functioning efficiently if, as is the case in France and Italy, over 20 per cent of its voters regularly support an alienated protest group like the Communist party; and where from an additional 10 per cent (Italy) to 25 per cent (France) support other "anti-constitutional" groups of the right or the left, anxiety is justified.[105] The defeat of de Gaulle and the election of Georges Pompidou as President do not appear to have reduced political alienation in France.

A peculiarity of French and Italian culture is the occasional resort to forms of extra-legal or even illegal referenda. It is not improbable that the high degree of political alienation in these countries induces the people to turn to extra-legal methods of expression of opinion. In France the favorite forms are the general strike and the barricade. The syndicalist tradition in the French labor movement has helped to build up the favorable image the general strike has in the minds of many Frenchmen, as has its use in support of many popular causes.[106] An unusual example was the positive strike in favor of de Gaulle at the time of the aborted Algerian *putsch*. In this case, the strikers expressed their support of the government by abstaining from work. Barricades also serve as popular demonstrations for political purposes. The essential

[105] See Gabriel A. Almond and Sidney Verba, *The Civic Culture* (Princeton: Princeton University Press, 1963), for further examples of political alienation in Italy. For France, see Herbert Lüthy, *France Against Herself* (New York: Frederick A. Praeger, Inc., 1955), and the daily press.

[106] See Val E. Lorwin, *The French Labor Movement* (Cambridge, Mass.: Harvard University Press, 1954), particularly ch. 3.

characteristic of both the general strike and the barricade is their high degree of spontaneity. Organized groups may plot them, encourage them and attempt to control them, but the size, temper, and determination of these demonstrations is quite unpredictable, and they are about as nearly an expression of general will of the social groups that effect them as one can ever find in large social systems.

The Italian pattern is somewhat different. There the typical instrument through which *vox populi* speaks is the "row in *piazza*." [107] Whenever the Italians are aroused, it is their traditional practice to demonstrate in the important squares of their cities. These demonstrations are essentially pacific. The mood, though one of anger, distrust, and disgust, spends itself in expression rather than rationally directed action. Rioting may get out of hand and a few deaths may result, but the whole attitude is somewhere between a protest and a temper tantrum and does not usually degenerate into looting and general subversion.

The Anglo-American and above all the German may wonder what possible effect such disorganized, undirected, and unfocused activity could have. But however unlikely it may seem to the more orderly northern European, these demonstrations are effective. Italy entered World War I, accepted fascism, and overthrew a Christian Democrat government relying on neo-fascist support (in 1963), each as a result of rows in *piazza*. The general strike and the student barricades of May, 1968, led to the fall of de Gaulle ten months later.

In spite of alienation in France and Italy, however, both cultures have shed blood for democracy. In Germany, on the other hand, there is respect for and an attitude of obedience toward the state, but little consideration in either sense of the word is given to parliament. Germany and Austria are alone among the liberal democracies in that the people have never fought for their freedom but rather have had it bestowed on them as a sort of punishment for losing wars.

Another significant distinction among liberal democratic po-

[107] I am indebted to George Macaulay Trevelyan for this concept. See G. M. Trevelyan, *The Historical Causes for the Present State of Affairs in Italy* (London: Oxford University Press, 1925).

litical systems relates to the role they assign the opposition. The British pattern of a loyal opposition that functions as a part of the formal government structure[108] is followed more or less loosely in the major English-speaking states and in Denmark and Norway. The Danish four-party system tends to form itself into two two-party coalitions that alternate in office (Det Konservative Folkeparti and Venstre, or Socialdemokratiet and Det radikale Venstre). In Norway, in order to end the long reign of the Labor Party (Arbeiderpartiet), the four other major parties were forced into what may well be a long-enduring coalition. This system seems to work in societies where there is a broad consensus on basic constitutional questions and where an election is treated almost as a sporting event, giving the victor the right to rule.

In the Netherlands, Belgium, and Italy, the Catholic center offers a stability to government against which an effective opposition is virtually impossible and the mildly anticlerical "liberal" right alternates in the government coalition with the mildly socialist left. Thus the Dutch Catholic Party and the Italian Democrazia cristiana have been continuously in power since World War II. The Parti social chrétien of Belgium and the Dutch Protestant parties, the Kristlijk Historische Unie and the Anti-Revolutionaire Partij (still fighting the French Revolution!), have formed part of the government coalition about 75 per cent of the time during this period. The CDU in Germany remained in power from the inception of the Bonn government until 1969, when a socialist and liberal coalition dethroned it, thus seeming to put Germany finally into the Anglo-American-Scandinavian two-party loyal opposition camp.

In Switzerland, the opposition is virtually eliminated by the present system of including the four major parties, which represent over 85 per cent of the vote, on the seven-man Federal Council. Lack of opposition means lack of competition. Thus in the canton of Uri no election for the Federal Assembly was held for over a generation, as the parties agreed to split the seats among themselves, giving the two seats in the Conseil des états to the Catholics and the single seat in the Conseil national to the

---

[108] See Max Beloff, "The Leader of the Opposition," *Parliamentary Affairs,* XI (1957-58), 155-162.

Radicals.[109] The Swiss system incorporates the basic elements of Calhoun's theory of the concurrent majority,[110] which is roughly the system of the Quakers' meeting, where people sit around waiting until consensus is reached through mutual compromise. If carried to the extreme this system leads to the *liberum veto*, by which any measure can be defeated by a single negative vote. The liberum veto was influential in destroying Polish parliamentarianism, and on the international scene it has been the bane of the United Nations and the European Common Market. The filibuster in the United States Senate, the instrument through which one or two determined senators can effectively thwart the will of the majority, is a sort of *de facto* liberum veto. If applied with moderation and common sense, government without opposition is a government of compromise; anarchy results if minority interests are repeatedly intransigent.

Although the elimination of an opposition seems to have produced no ill effects in Switzerland, it is not a foolproof system. Lebanon, sometimes called the Switzerland of the Near East, has continuously operated under this system, apparently so that all may share in the graft with no one in a position to start a scandal. In some American states and cities there is an informal agreement between the parties to eliminate effective opposition, under which the majority party offers patronage crumbs to the minority party in return for acquiescence to major plunder by the majority.[111]

Sweden alone of the liberal democracies has developed into something approaching a one-party system on a national scale. The Social Democratic Labor Party (Arbetarepartiet socialdemokratarna) has been in power continuously for over a third of a century, most of the time governing alone, but occasionally in coalition.

It has not been possible to establish a loyal opposition in any of the states described above where there has been a party with

[109] Hughes, *op. cit.*, pp. 37–51.

[110] John C. Calhoun, *Disquisition on Government* (1853), written five to ten years earlier). For some of the effects of this system, see George E. G. Catlin, "Septicentenarian Parliament," *Political Studies*, XIV (1966), 191–199.

[111] See, for example, Lockhart, *op. cit.*, ch. 8, which deals with Rhode Island.

a sectarian religious basis. Religious parties are almost exclusively
Roman Catholic or Calvinist. The only Lutheran party of consequence, the Kristelig Folkeparti of Norway, represents back-
woods, fundamentalist, teetotaling conservatism. The Lutherans
of Sweden and Denmark and the Zwingliites of Switzerland have
no political parties. The CDU of Germany attempts to attract
both Roman Catholics and Lutherans and appears quite independent of church control.

Religion plays a special role in Lebanese politics, where by
convention different government posts are assigned to the various sects, of which the five most important are the Maronites
(affiliated with the Roman Catholic Church), the Greek Orthodox, the Sunni Moslems, the Shiite Moslems, and the Druze.
According to this convention, the president of the Republic
must be a Maronite, the prime minister a Sunni, the president
of the chamber a Shiite, the minister of war a Druze, and the
commanding general a Maronite or other Christian. The result
of this convention is that political competition is limited much
as it is in Switzerland.

Only France and Italy have large disloyal oppositions. In the
Fifth Republic, de Gaulle enjoyed the support of a comfortable
majority of his compatriots for some years even though there was
also an unhealthily large, alienated and revolutionary minority.
Since the breakup of this majority and de Gaulle's subsequent
retirement, the situation has become too fluid for brief analysis.
The major distinction between the French and Italian situations
lies in the role played by the Democrazia cristiana, which has
been consistently the largest vote-getter and the dominant member of the government coalition in post-war Italy. The Christian
Democracy thus ranks just behind the Radical, Catholic and
Agrarian parties of Switzerland, the Swedish socialists, and the
Dutch Catholics as the party to be represented in the government
for the longest continuous period. This has given a remarkable
stability to Italian government quite lacking in France, assuring
governmental continuity and acting as a focal point for the *status
quo* (some would say the *status quo ante*).

In France, the vestiges of a syndicalist tradition in the trade
union movement keep the labor leaders out of parliament. The

representative nature of the French parliament is influenced by the habit of electing mayors to the national legislature. Édouard Herriot, the Radical leader, was the perennial mayor of the large city of Lyon for over half a century, during which time he served in parliament and in many cabinets, and even held the position of premier on several occasions. The custom of electing mayors as deputies serves as a counterbalance to the préfect in France. The former assures local influence in Paris; the latter, the influence of the central government throughout the various levels of local government.[112]

What may be a misguided sense of the requirements of modern democracy has caused Italy to ban the practice of having mayors sit in parliament. There is logic in the argument that being mayor and being a member of parliament are both full-time jobs, but it is also true that local government in such highly centralized governments as those of France and Italy has a real need of an authoritative voice in the capital. If Lyon was willing to offer both positions simultaneously to Herriot for virtually a lifetime, if Bordeaux is still content to give both posts to Jacques Chaban-Delmas, and Marseilles continues to do the same with Gaston Deferre, it would seem there must be a reason, and if there is one it should apply equally to Italy. The rapport between local and central government is institutionalized in Germany by the Bundesrat, the members of which are the responsible Länder executives.

The Servicing of Legislators

In many states (e.g., Great Britain, Sweden, Switzerland), the drafting of legislation is virtually a monopoly of the executive. In states like France, where skeletal legislation is the tradition, the flesh is added by administrative decree to a statute that may

---

[112] See, for example, De Tarr, *op. cit.*, and Brian Chapman, *Introduction to French Local Government* (London: Allen & Unwin, Ltd., 1953).

have set down little more than the scope of a proposed policy and the end it seeks to attain. Such states normally have a bill-drafting agency in the executive that is responsible for the language of the bill.

In the United States, the practice is to have a bill-drafting agency directly servicing the legislature. This is a virtual necessity, given the large number of private member bills. The fact that such a service is not available to Italian legislators, who also introduce a large number of private member bills, explains in good part the frequency of badly drafted legislation in Italy.

There is a vast difference from state to state in the amount of senatorial and research assistance supplied to legislators. No other country is as generous as the United States in staffing its representatives with secretaries and special service agencies. This helps to make the Congress, and the legislatures of those of the states that follow the federal pattern, the center of an activity that in other countries either is not carried out or is done in other ways. The secretarial help afforded American congressmen makes possible the handling of quantities of correspondence. The British MP, in contrast, has no paid secretary and until recently he did not even have an office. In systems in which a representative cannot count on all-out or effective support of his national party for his biennial election campaigns, as, for example, the American and French systems, fan and other mail from constituents must be treated seriously.[113] The British MP appears somewhat less dependent on such services in order to secure reelection.

Most legislative bodies have libraries attached to them. Many of these libraries (e.g., the libraries of the Swiss parliament and of the Italian Senate, and, if one can count so independent a body, the Library of Congress) are excellent. In some instances, however, the legislator has less use for books, which he may have no time to read, than for research assistants, who can get him the facts. One of the major leverages of the pressure groups on

---

[113] See Marie-Thérèse Lancelot, "Le courrier d'un parlementaire," *Revue française de science politique*, XII (1962), 426–432, for an analysis of the mail received by a French deputy.

parliament in some countries is their ability to supply the deputies with pertinent information that the deputies are unable to obtain by themselves. Here again the American legislator is the best off.

Nonlegislative Functions of Parliament

No valid evaluation of the effectiveness of parliament in the legislative process can be undertaken without examining the services parliament performs outside its involvement with this process. Although they lie beyond the scope of this book, it is appropriate to mention the more important services here and to show their relationship to parliament's efficiency as a legislative body, because it is as a by-product of such activities that parliament becomes better prepared to carry out its legislative function.

As we have seen, the traditional functions of parliament were being carried out centuries before there was any sustained effort on its part to operate as a legislative body. Among these functions were those of protecting the interest of the public against the administration, and of acting as a forum for communication between the government and the people for the purpose of forming and formulating public opinion.

Parliament has relied on certain basic techniques for the performance of these functions. They include the question period, the investigatory committee, and the establishment of specific procedures and offices for the control of executive action. Other procedures, such as impeachment and the adoption of resolutions and motions, may also be used, but do not appear to call for comment here.

Members of parliament ask questions of the officers of the government for various reasons. The method of presenting the question is likely to vary with the purpose in asking it. If the purpose is to correct a minor administrative error or injustice, then a private letter from the member to the responsible administrative officer is generally most efficacious. This velvet glove approach is appreciated by the administration, but it scarcely hides the fact that where compliance is not forthcoming the administration is likely to be faced with a possibly embarrassing formal question on the same subject.

A formal question is the approved method when the member is more concerned with publicity than with results. If the question concerns a minor matter, the questioner may be content with a written answer from the ministry. When an opposition deputy has an embarrassing question to ask, he is likely to ask for an oral reply from the minister. In some liberal democratic systems, the deputy may ask further supplementary questions arising out of the minister's answer. The right to ask supplementary questions is treasured by the British members of parliament, and much of the drama and publicity of British parliamentary life stems from the skill with which questions are asked and parried at Westminster Hall.[114]

When parliament is seriously concerned over the action of the government, it uses the technique of the question to condemn the government. This type of question is generally called an interpellation on the European continent. In England, it is called an adjournment debate. Such a debate results from a motion generally arising from the inability of the government to give a satisfactory answer to an oral question. The motion, which must be supported by 40 members and must have the approval of the speaker on the grounds that it refers to an urgent, important, and definite issue, proposes that at 7 P.M. of the same day parliament should adjourn its regular business and debate this issue.

A question is essentially a fact stated interrogatively ("Is the Minister of Education aware that . . . ?") calling the attention of the administration to a grievance. An interpellation or an adjournment debate is a call on the government for a general accounting on a given issue and may lead to a motion of censure. Any member of parliament may ask either kind of question in

[114] See Frank Stacey, *The Government of Modern Britain* (Oxford: Clarendon Press, 1968), pp. 110–120.

Belgium, Denmark, Italy, the Netherlands, Norway,[115] Sweden,[116] and Switzerland. This right is exercised frequently in Belgium and Italy, but is less commonly employed in the Scandinavian countries and the Netherlands. In Germany and France, questions but not interpellations may be presented by a single member. Thirty deputies must sign an interpellation in Germany, and the procedure for reply is so cumbersome that the number of interpellations presented is steadily declining.[117] The French parliament is forbidden to discuss the general policy of the government except through the procedure of the vote of censure, which may be unavailable or inappropriate.

The United States lacks this procedure on both the national and the state level. The investigatory committee replaces the major interpellations, and the threat of formal questions that backs up the European representatives' informal requests for redress of grievances is replaced by the fear of other, somewhat vaguer reprisals usually connected with the power of the purse.

Parliament may exercise control over the administration by appointing inspectors to examine administrative activity and report to the legislature. A common field of operation for such inspectors is the post audit; another is civil rights. Controls of this nature not only discourage and remedy administrative abuses; they also keep parliament informed of administrative problems and practices. The members of an informed parliament are obviously in a better position to make a valid contribution to the legislative process.

Fiscal controls in the nature of a post audit are entrusted in Great Britain to a parliamentary inspector called the comptroller and auditor general. He is an officer of parliament, paid by it and removable by it alone. He is usually an ex-treasury officer, who is familiar with the principles and practices of government accounting. His primary function is to examine the public ac-

[115] See Nona Bowring, "On Asking Questions in the Norwegian Parliament," *Political Studies*, X (1962), 284–287.

[116] The Riksdagman must make a pro forma request to his house for permission to make an interpellation. See Andrén, *op. cit.*, pp. 91–92.

[117] Loewenberg, *op. cit.*, pp. 408–409.

counts in order to determine that allotted money was spent for the purposes intended and in an efficient and economical manner. He reports the results of his audit to the parliamentary Select Committee on Public Accounts. This committee convenes annually when the comptroller and auditor general gives his report, and it has the power to call witnesses. All in all, it appears to be a reasonably effective check on government spending. Part of the reason for its prestige and success may lie in the convention that its chairman be a member of the opposition.

A similar system operates in New Zealand,[118] and after a nineteen-year hiatus one started up again in Australia in 1951.[119] Canada, however, has only the shell of the system, with little effective parliamentary control. There, the committee meets only when the comptroller and auditor general has discovered some scandalous skulduggery. It further differs from the British system in that its chairman is a member of the government majority.[120]

In Switzerland, the Federal Council is required to submit an annual post audit to parliament. Parliament in turn has established a six-man *Délégation des finances,* composed of three members of the finance committee of each house, which gives a thorough examination to the Council's report. Membership in the delegation is a prestige appointment for members of parliament. The parliamentary expert in financial control is the delegation's secretary; this man is also the secretary for the finance committees of both houses and for the *Contrôle des finances* of the Finance Department of the Federal Council; he thus sits at the juncture between the legislature and the administration.[121]

The French and Italian post audit is entrusted to special audit courts, the Cour des comptes and the Corte dei conti. Although the reports of these agencies are submitted to parliament, the

[118] See Leslie Lipson, *The Politics of Equality* (Chicago: University of Chicago Press, 1948), pp. 326–327.

[119] Alexander Brady, *Democracy in the Dominions* (3d ed., Toronto: University of Toronto Press, 1958), p. 188.

[120] *Ibid.,* pp. 78–79.

[121] Marcel Bridel, *Précis de droit constitutionnel et public suisse, Deuxième partie, Les organes de l'état* (Lausanne: Payot, 1959), pp. 80, 90; and Hughes, *op. cit.,* pp. 142–144.

submission generally occurs years after the fact, and the parliaments have set up no machinery for acting on these matters. The American General Accounting Office is probably a more efficient organization, but it too operates independently of Congress. The Italian and American legislators, however, have ample occasion to learn about fiscal matters in discussing and approving the budget, while members of the French parliament, who can neither cut receipts nor increase taxes, have little effect on fiscal policy.[122]

Although the Swedish Justitieombudsman was originally an officer appointed by the crown and charged with protecting the interests of the crown, the present-day ombudsmen are all creatures of parliament charged with protecting civil liberties. After his appointment by the Riksdag, however, the Swedish ombudsman is virtually independent. He receives complaints directly from the public, and in the rare cases when it becomes necessary, he initiates legal proceedings.

The Danish and Norwegian ombudsmen likewise receive complaints directly from the public, but they have only advisory powers and refer all unsettled matters to parliament. The New Zealand and British ombudsmen, on the other hand, are strictly parliamentary agents. They are competent to examine only the cases referred to them by members of parliament and have only advisory powers. As in Denmark and Norway, differences of opinion between the ombudsman and the administration are referred to parliament for action.

It is apparent that the relationship between parliament and the ombudsman differs significantly from state to state. While the Riksdag seems to have delegated considerable power and responsibility to the ombudsman, the New Zealanders and the British keep him very much the servant of parliament. In each case, however, the ombudsman is a valid adjunct to parliament in carrying out its vital watchdog function. At the same time, through his annual reports and in some systems his individual case reports, he serves another perhaps equally important function, that of keeping parliament informed of the kinds of ques-

[122] Ludovic Tron, "Loi de finances et parlement," *Revue politique et parlementaire* (September, 1963), pp. 20–24.

tions over which conflicts arise between the administration and the citizen.

Having completed this brief assessment of the various liberal democratic parliaments, we turn next to an evaluation of parliament as legislator. Chapter 5 presents the negative side of the picture; in the last chapter, a defense of parliament will be offered.

5.

THE DISILLUSIONMENT WITH PARLIAMENT IN LIBERAL DEMOCRACIES:

A Descent from the Hill of Dreams to the Quagmire of Reality

Recent Opinions on Parliament

Since parliament is the formal source of law in liberal democracies, and the instrument through which the will of the sovereign people is formulated, liberal democrats presumably would have a great respect for parliament and would elect the best citizens to the high office of deputy, while legislative enactments would be received with deference or even awe. Yet even a cursory examination shows that this is not the case.

Here is what two eminent students of the American political scene had to say about Congress and the American legislatures in general:

> Congress, we are told, is the heart of representative government, the citadel of American democracy. Such a claim is more an expression of faith than a statement of fact.[1]
>
> The procedures of American legislatures defy effective public scrutiny and control . . . legislatures [are] the most backward,

[1] James M. Burns, *Congress on Trial* (New York: Harper & Row, 1949), p. 49.

incompetent, and machine-ruled of our institutions. They are filled with small fry, ranging from nice young lawyers supplementing incomes from incipient practices to party hacks who diligently do the bidding of invisible masters, and a few devoted senior habitués who know the business and make a small, ill-paid profession of the service.[2]

And a thoughtful American senator added:

It is the third branch of government, the legislature, where things have gone awry. Whether we look at city councils, the state legislatures, or the Congress of the United States, we react to what we see with scarcely concealed contempt. . . .

As a former chief executive of a large American city, as a member of the United States Senate, as a public servant who, in both capacities, has been obliged to know a good deal about the workings of state government, I have no hesitation in stating my deep conviction that the legislatures of America, local, state, and national, are presently the greatest menace in our country to the successful operation of the democratic process.[3]

Even the "mother of parliaments" is not immune from this general dissatisfaction. The following comment is taken almost at random from contemporary discussions of the British legislature:

The Commons vote last Thursday against broadcasting its

[2] Richard S. Childs, *Civic Victories* (New York: Harper & Row, 1953), pp. 117–118.

[3] Joseph S. Clark, *Congress: The Sapless Branch* (New York: Harper & Row, 1964), pp. 22–23. There is no end of material corroborating this view. Two recent symposia on the role of Congress, the discussions at which have been published as *The Congress and America's Future*, ed. David Truman (Englewood Cliffs, N.J.: Prentice-Hall, Inc., 1966), and *Congress: The First Branch of Government*, ed. Alfred de Grazia (Washington, D.C.: The American Enterprise Institute for Public Policy Research, 1966), attest to the general concern in the United States over the performance of Congress. On the state level, see, for instance, Duane Lockhart, *New England State Politics* (Princeton, N.J.: Princeton University Press, 1959), and for the old-fashioned muckraking techniques, Warren Boroson, "The State Legislatures as a Two-Ring Circus," *Fact*, II, 6 (1965), 41–47.

own proceedings represents a new low in the tragic decline of British parliamentary government. Indeed the term has ceased to have any meaning. Parliament today does not govern nor does it have any significant control over the people who do.[4]

And a well-known British political commentator, Bernard Levin, was quoted as saying: "The House of Commons today is in a state of decay, incompetence, and fully justified ill repute worse than at any time since the worst days of George III." [5]

In the larger states of western Europe, where there are meager traditions of effective parliamentary government, attitudes are still more negative. After seventy years of rule, marked by scandal, corruption, ineffectiveness, and inefficiency, the parliamentary government of France's Third Republic ingloriously abdicated and entrusted its powers to Pétain, a reactionary who appeared to repudiate not only the revolutions of 1870, 1848, and 1830, but that of 1789 as well. The parliament of the Fourth Republic, established in 1945 after the Vichy interlude under Pétain, was as ineffective as that of the Third. Not only was the government of the Third Republic discredited but so were the majority of the governors; thus the institutions of the Fourth Republic, for the most part unrefurbished replicas of those of the Third, and the majority of its political figures, besmirched by the cowardice of the abdication to Pétain, failed to gain the respect, the confidence, or even the good will of the French public. The death of the Fourth Republic was more ignominious than that of the Third. It collapsed not under the pressure of a military defeat but from the apathy of the public and its own utter inability to face problems and reach decisions. The acceptance of de Gaulle and of the constitution of the Fifth Republic were indications that the French cared little for liberal democracy in 1958. By his subsequent actions de Gaulle continued to show contempt for parliament, while even his many

[4] John Grigg, "Decline of the Commons," *Manchester Guardian Weekly*, December 1, 1966, p. 6.

[5] *Newsweek*, November 7, 1966, p. 54. See also Bernard Crick, *The Reform of Parliament: The Crisis of British Government in the 1960's* (London: Weidenfeld & Nicolson, Ltd., 1964).

opponents and detractors in France showed little enthusiasm for a return to parliamentary government.[6] With the fall of de Gaulle in 1969 and the establishment of what is sometimes called the Fifth and a Half Republic (*le république cinquième bis*) under the presidency of Georges Pompidou and the premiership of Jacques Chaban-Delmas, former president of the Assemblée nationale, parliament, for the moment, has been treated with greater consideration.

The Italian dissatisfaction with parliament dates back at least to Gaetano Mosca. The ineffectiveness of the parliamentary system in the face of fascism, both before and after the march on Rome, further undermined the prestige of parliament. With the fall of fascism and the reestablishment of parliamentary democracy, this prestige rose again, and the generally high caliber of the men Italy sent to her Constituent Assembly and her first Republican parliament further enhanced parliament in the eyes of the public. This promising first impression, however, was soon canceled by parliament's poor performance and the consistently lower caliber of deputies and senators elected to subsequent parliaments. Since then one rarely hears a good word for the Italian parliament from scholars, journalists, or the public at large.

The complaints focus on such major issues as parliament's unwillingness to implement many provisions of the constitution by enabling legislation, its peculiar and undemocratic procedures—such as secret voting and committee legislation—and the inordinate amount of time it consumes in passing *leggine* (miniscule amendments to general laws), usually intended to extend some privilege to a small and insistent vested interest.[7]

The history of Germany is that of a people who have cared little for freedom and who have gained little from asserting

----

[6] See, for example, Albert Mabileau, "La personalisation du pouvoir dans les gouvernements démocratiques," *Revue française de science politique*, X (1960), 39–65; Édouard Bertrand de Jouvenel des Ursins, "Du principat," *ibid.*, XIV (1964), 1053–1086; and Jacques Vrignaud, "Quel avenir pour les parlements?", *Revue politique et parlementaire* (January, 1966), 65–83.

[7] See, for example, Alberto Predieri, "Per l'introduzione delle udienze legislative nel parlamento italiano," *Il ponte*, XXII (1960), 1109–1126. See

their rights. They have normally obeyed their leaders and have often benefited from the effective paternalism of their rulers. The German veneration for hierarchy and bureaucracy is not particularly compatible with the give-and-take of parliamentary debates. The fiasco of the Weimar Republic did not encourage the Germans to respect parliament. And although the success of the Bonn government has doubtless lessened the negative criticisms, parliament appears to have acquired little of the credit for the relatively smooth functioning of the state. Chancellor Adenauer himself governed in an essentially autocratic manner and showed little deference to the Bundestag.[8]

The Historical Liberal Opposition

Attitudes of derision and disrespect for parliament are almost as old as the institution of representative government. Criticisms have gone to the very heart of the parliamentary system, and are particularly disheartening when, as sometimes occurs, they come from the pens of persons fundamentally in sympathy with

---

also Giovanni Sartori (ed.), *Il parlamento in Italia* (particularly the article by Alberto Predieri); John Clarke Adams and Paolo Barile, *The Government of Republican Italy* (2d ed., Boston: Houghton Mifflin Company, 1966); and Federico Comandini, "Il parlamento ammalato," *Il ponte*, XVIII (1963), 637–658. As this book goes to press (1970), thorough but not very far-reaching revisions of the procedure of both houses of parliament have been proposed. The new Senate proposal is out of committee while the Chamber proposal is not. Neither proposal discards the practice of allowing final action on bills in committee or secret voting. Both propose electrical voting.

[8] For a recent and authoritative statement of this view, see Karl Jaspers, *Whither Goes the Federal Republic?* (Munich: R. Piper, 1966). See also Walter Euchner, "Zur lage des Parlamentarismus," in Stanzick, Euchner, Hinz, Bacia, Negt, *et al.*, *Der CDU-Staat. Studien zur Verfassungswirklichkeit der Bundesrepublik* (Munich: Sczesny Verlag, 1967). The election of President Heineman and Chancellor Brandt in 1969, both socialists, promises a significant policy change in Germany, but it may have little effect on the role of parliament.

the liberal philosophy. Some of the most authoritative of the early critics were liberal deputies in their respective countries and therefore not only favorably disposed to liberal democracy but cognizant of the inner workings of parliament. Mosca, as early as 1877, predicted that the parliamentary systems of France and Italy were headed for a rapid demise.[9] Mosca believed that in the modern state, parliamentary government cannot be truly representative.[10] The successful candidate must be willing to be the tool of the bosses (*grandi elettori*) and to pander to the prejudices of the mob. He argued that a majority view rarely exists, as the majority is usually either uninterested and poorly informed about issues or incapable of making its opinions felt because it is usually poorly organized. When the voters are organized, the politicians who did the organizing have probably prostituted themselves by the use of rabble-rousing tactics and by the espousal of a socially harmful program adapted to the greed and stupidity of the mob.

Mosca draws examples from his observations of Italian politics and from numerous French, Italian, and American sources. He has little criticism of the British parliament but holds that it is not exportable. He does, however, assert that the British government was most corrupt during the first fifty years of parliamentary government, which he places in the eighteenth century under the first two Georges.[11]

One of the most brilliant analyses of the disfunctioning of parliament comes from the French aristocratic liberal Charles Benoist, and is based for the most part on his long experience with and in French politics. It is probable that nowhere in the

[9] "Che possa e debba durare lungamente il regime parlamentare quale l'abbiamo ora in Italia, quale è in Francia . . . che esso possa quindi divenire una forma di Governo stabile e normale noi non crediamo in niun modo probabile"—Mosca, *Teorica*, Conclusion.

[10] Mosca, *Le costituzioni moderne*, ch. 3, sec. 4.

[11] Mosca, *Teorica*, ch. 6, sec. 8. See also Marco Minghetti, *I partiti politici e la pubblica amministrazione* (Bologna, 1881; reprinted Bologna: Cappelli, 1969). For the opinions of nineteenth-century southern Italian political leaders, see Massimo Salvadori, *Il mito del buon governo* (Torino: Einaudi, 1960).

West has parliament produced such poor results over so long a period as in France. Writing at the end of the nineteenth century, Benoist had this to say of parliament:

> If there is a single point in the thorny matter of politics . . . where agreement is possible today . . . it is that things are in a bad way. . . . Parliament does and undoes, calls for a government and then either blocks it from governing or overthrows it, affirms and denies, rushes into the fray and then passes the buck, acclaims and anathematizes. France is not represented, nothing is accomplished, and it is hard to say which is most upsetting, the convulsions of parliament or the agony of the nation.[12]

In a series of essays written for the *Revue des deux mondes* after World War I, Benoist urges us to

> look at the deputies we elect. . . . Look at what they are and remember what they do. In three great and terrible words, they "make the law." Do they know what the law is and how it is made? Not they! Most of them have not even the foggiest conception of it. A short time ago one was in his shop, another at his desk, others were haranguing trade union meetings, or hanging around the bars. A combination of chance and intrigue brings them to parliament. Improvised as they are, they in turn improvise.[13]

In these essays Benoist attempts to isolate the diseases endemic to parliamentary government. Three of them deserve special mention here. Parliamentitis occurs when large, poorly selected parliamentary bodies meet for one or more daily sessions through-

---

[12] Benoist, *La crise de l'état moderne,* pp. 1–2.

[13] "Examinez bien, je vous prie, ces gens qui vont s'asseoir sur les banquettes. . . . Voyez ce qu'ils sont et rappelez-vous ce qu'ils font. En trois syllabes, immenses et terribles, ils 'font la loi'. Ils savent donc ce que sont les lois et comment se font les lois? Eux! Les huit dixièmes ne s'en doutent même pas. L'un était hier à son officine, l'autre à son bureau, le troisième à son établi, et plusieurs, en outre, péroraient dans les syndicats ou traînaient dans les cafés. Le jeu de l'intrigue et du hasard en a fait des législateurs. Improvisés, ils improvisent"—*Les maladies,* pp. 14–15.

out most of the year. Under these conditions, the individual personalities of the deputies dissolve physically and morally in the overheated atmosphere and amalgamate into a type of "parliamentary man" far below the mediocre average of the individual members of parliament.[14] Electionitis, prevalent wherever a government is elected, requires the deputy to pander to the voters' passions and prejudices. In electing him, "the voters open an account with him with a large credit balance and during the four years of his mandate they will expect to collect all types of favors, job preferences, and public recognition." [15] Furthermore, in a parliamentary democracy there are no criteria of selection, and anyone may be called at any time and sent anywhere, to do anything in whatever way he can. These are the symptoms of the third disease, n'importequisme, which might be translated as indiscriminativitis.

Although the entire parliamentary system feels the lash of Benoist's passionate invective, his basic argument, as was the case with Mosca, is that the system is an importation from Great Britain not suitable to the "Latin" countries.[16] British writers have agreed with Benoist on this point. A traditional source is Sir William Blackstone who, it is claimed, in speaking of the rights of man said he really meant the rights of Englishmen.[17] John Stuart Mill warns us twice[18] that parliamentary government will work only under three conditions: If the people (1) want it, (2) are able to operate it, and (3) are capable of enabling it to achieve its ends. Walter Bagehot expressed the same idea in more sophisticated terms by giving as the three requisites of liberal democracy: (1) the mutual confidence of the electors, (2) a calm national mind, and (3) ration-

[14] *Ibid.,* pp. 11–12.

[15] ". . . ses électeurs lui ont ouvert un compte qui part pour lui d'un lourd débit. Ils inscriront en regard, dans les quatre ans qui lui sont accordés, les bénéfices, emplois, faveurs, décorations, passedroits de toute sorte qu'il leur rapportera"—*ibid.,* p. 20.

[16] *Ibid.,* pp. 26, 27.

[17] I have not found this remark in a cursory look through the *Commentaries,* but its spirit pervades his chapter on rights.

[18] *Representative Government* (1860), chs. 1 and 4.

ality. These qualities lead to the creation of a "deferential nation," that is, "one in which the numerous unwiser part wishes to be ruled by the less numerous wiser part." He found all these attributes missing in "the peculiar mores of semi-barbarous people," which he characterized as "diffused distrust and indiscriminate suspicion." [19] In another place Bagehot expressed essentially the same thought with laconic English wit: "I fear you will laugh when I tell you what I conceive to be the most essential quality for a free people, whose liberty is to be progressive, permanent, and on a large scale; it is much stupidity . . . I need not say that in real sound stupidity the English are unrivaled . . ." [20]

Rightists have been attracted by this view. Curzio Malaparte, for instance, uses it as a basis for one of the most intelligent apologies for fascism, contending that the Risorgimento imposed a foreign system—representative democracy—on Italy. (According to Malaparte, fascism was the truly Italian government that Italians had wanted all along.) [21] And Guglielmo Ferrero put it this way:

> Most of the parliaments set up in Europe in the nineteenth century were abortive because they did not represent true majorities but camouflaged and antagonistic minorities. . . . All too often they developed into centers of fraud and violence contrived to subvert the will of the voters by creating false majorities and by suppressing the right of opposition.[22]

The American congress and the state legislatures have not been free of similar criticisms. The Russian liberal M. I. Ostrogorski, after strongly criticizing the congress, has this to say of the states:

[19] *The English Constitution* (1867), ch. 9. See also Alan Burns (ed.), *Parliament as an Export* (London: Allen & Unwin, Ltd., 1966).

[20] Walter Bagehot, "Letters on the French Coup d'Etat," in *Literary Studies,* cited in Jacques Barzun, *The House of Intellect* (New York: Harper & Row, 1959), p. 148.

[21] *Italia barbara* (Turin: Gobetti, 1925).

[22] Guglielmo Ferrero, *Pouvoir, les génies invisibles de la cité* (New York: Brentano's, 1942), p. 190.

> The State legislatures exhibit in a still greater degree the decline, one would be almost entitled to say the collapse, of representative government. . . . The finances are administered without regard for economy. . . . The laws are made with singular incompetence and carelessness. . . . The motions which enter into the making of these laws are often of an obviously mercenary nature.[23]

Professions of this general opinion became even more common in the twenties after the world had been made "safe for democracy" by the Allied victory in 1918. H. L. Mencken, America's favorite iconoclast of the twenties, expressed in his highly personal way the pseudo-sophisticated view of his age. After the general comment that "the . . . result is a House of Representatives that, in intelligence, information and integrity, is comparable to a gang of bootleggers—a House so deficient in competent leaders that it can scarcely carry on its business," he moved on to one of his major *bêtes noires,* the Southern congressman:

> The average Southern member, for example . . . got his early education in a hedge school, he proceeded to some preposterous Methodist or Baptist college, and then he served for a time as a school teacher in his native swamps. . . . The unfitness of such a man for the responsibilities of a law maker must be obvious. Having to choose between sense and nonsense, he chooses nonsense almost instinctively. Until he got to Washington and began to meet lobbyists, bootleggers and correspondents of the newspapers, he had perhaps never met a single intelligent human being. As a Congressman he remains below the salt. Officialdom disclaims him, he is kept waiting in anterooms by all the fourth assistant secretaries. When he is invited to a party it is a sign that police sergeants are also invited. . . . His dream is to be chosen to go on a congressional junket, i.e., on a drunken holiday at government expense. . . . It is such vermin who make the laws of the United States.[24]

[23] Moisei Iakoflovich Ostrogorski, *Democracy and the Organization of Political Parties* (New York: The Macmillan Company, 1908), Part V, ch. 10, sec. 11.

[24] H. L. Mencken, *Notes on Democracy* (London: Jonathan Cape, Ltd., 1927), pp. 134–136.

A striking contrast to this flamboyant invective is Lord Bryce's measured understatement:

> There is evidence to indicate in nearly every country some decline from that admiration of and confidence in the system of representative government which in England possessed the generation who took their constitutional history from Hallam and Macaulay and their political philosophy from John Stuart Mill and Walter Bagehot.[25]

And the distinguished American professor of political theory, George Sabine, agreed with this:

> The fact is that as representative assemblies have become matter of course we have very generally lost confidence in them as organs for making law. . . . If anything is written large across the histories of our states, it is popular distrust of the Legislature. Our State constitutions, with their detailed restrictions upon legislative power, are monuments to this distrust.[26]

Parties and Pressure Groups

Other writers, while supporting the principles of liberal democracy, have turned their ire on certain political realities which the theorists had not taken into account. Thus parties and lobbies have each been the object of proliferous abuse.

Liberal democratic theorists were aware of the danger of parties, although they generally used the term "factions." James Harrington insisted that in his ideal commonwealth, "there should be no laying of heads together, conventicals or canvassing

---

[25] James Bryce, *Modern Democracies* (12 vols., New York: The Macmillan Company, 1921), Vol. II, p. 335.

[26] George H. Sabine, "What Is the Matter with Representative Government?," *North American Review,* CCXIII (1921), 587–597, cited in Christensen and Kirkpatrick, *op. cit.,* p. 404.

to carry on or oppose anything." [27] Rousseau was equally alarmed
that through the formation of factions his elixir of democracy,
la volonté générale, would become denatured into a *volonté de
tous*—a sum of the selfish interests.[28] James Madison added his
warning on the need "to break and control the violence of faction." [29]

In spite of these warnings and premonitions, however, the public in liberal democracies seemed shocked and alarmed at the
advent of political parties, which were nothing but a species of
faction, and a negative reaction was not slow to develop. It was
primarily one of alarm and concern over the misuse of the power
they wielded. Some of the alarm was partisan, but much of it
attained the support of a virtual consensus. Thus the power of
Jefferson's political machine and its tactics aroused the anger
and dismay of the Federalists and of conservatives in general,
and the power and tactics of Jackson's machine provoked perhaps an even stronger reaction on the part of the conservatives of
the following generation, one that went beyond the attack on a
man to become an attack on a system. By the post-Civil War
period, the power of the party so distorted the constitutional system in the United States that Charles E. Merriam wrote: "In
every section of the country and at all times in this period the
extra-legal and unofficial agency known as the party to a very
large extent took the place of the official agency known as the
government." [30] It is interesting to note that this is precisely the

[27] Charles Blitzer, *An Immortal Commonwealth* (New Haven, Conn.: Yale
University Press, 1960), p. 240.

[28] Jean Jacques Rousseau, *Du contrat social* (Amsterdam, 1762).

[29] *The Federalist,* No. X.

[30] Charles E. Merriam, *American Political Ideas* (New York: The Macmillan Company, 1920), p. 270. Interesting early accounts of the influence of
party on politics are found in the Anglo-American literature of the nineteenth
and twentieth centuries. Anthony Trollope (for example, *Ralph the Heir,
Phineas Finn, The Duke's Children*) and Benjamin Disraeli on the British
side and Winston Churchill (for example, *Coniston* [1906], *Mr. Crewe's
Career* [1908], *A Fair Country* [1915], *The Dwelling Place of Light* [1917])
on the American side are particularly recommended. The tradition has been
carried on by the later writers, including Eliot Paul (see *The Governor of
Massachusetts*). For a nonfictional diatribe against parties by another novelist,

criticism frequently directed at the totalitarian parties of the twentieth century.[31]

After the Second Reform Act of 1867, the British parties became sufficiently well organized under William Gladstone and Benjamin Disraeli to interfere obviously with the popular conception of the proper operation of parliamentary government. The effect of Gladstone's and Disraeli's work was apparent to Sir W. S. Gilbert in 1882, as well as to his delighted audiences. In that year Sergeant Willis first confided some of his "astonishing" thoughts to the public:

> I often think it comical
> How nature always does contrive
> That every boy and every gal
> That's born into this world alive
> Is either a little liberal
> Or else a little conservative.[32]

This fairly mild satire against political conformity is followed immediately by a far more cruel jibe at parliament:

> When in that house MP's divide
> If they've a brain and cerebellum, too,
> They've got to leave that brain outside
> And vote just as their leaders tell 'em to.
> But then the prospect of a lot
> Of dull MP's in close proximity
> All thinking for themselves is what
> No man can face with equanimity.[33]

The popular reaction in the United States continued for some time to be strongly anti-party. The reform movement directed its energies to the control of the parties. Among the reforms aimed

---

see the citation from James Fenimore Cooper quoted in John M. Swarthout and Ernest N. Bartley (eds.), *Materials on American National Government* (2d ed., New York: Oxford University Press, 1962), pp. 157–159.

[31] See, for example, Piero Calamandrei, *La funzione parlamentare sotto il fascismo* (Rome: Camera dei deputati, 1948).

[32] *Iolanthe*, Act II.

[33] *Ibid.*

at eliminating abuses arising out of the activities of the parties were the Pendleton Act, setting up a merit system in the civil service; the introduction of the Australian ballot; the movements for the short ballot, direct primaries, initiative, referendum, and recall; and statutes attempting to control party finance such as the Hatch Act. The British at the same time were writing their stringent legislation on election practices, dealing particularly with the limitation of and accountability for expenditures.

The enemies of strong parties have not been routed. They are still strong, particularly in France, Italy, and Germany. In these countries, an essentially negative approach has developed as a direct attack on parties that offers nothing to take their place. The Italians of this ilk call the present form of government in liberal democracies *partitocrazia* (party rule);[34] they offer the essentially reactionary solution of a return to parliamentary government. Apparently, they wish to recapture the parliamentary government of a virtually mythical England with attributes taken from the actual British governments of various periods, some before the 1832 Reform Bill, some after the 1867 Reform Bill, and some from the middle period. (One may infer that they dislike the present form of British liberal democracy, which is a partitocrazia *par excellence*.) Party rule, like any other form of government, is at its worst when it lacks the power to act effectively. The partitocrazie of France and Italy are bad forms of government, not because of the strength but because of the weakness of the parties in those countries.

When the cry against the parties died down, it was followed by equally virulent attacks against the "lobbies," the pressure groups sponsoring the "vested interests" against the general welfare. These attacks got under way in the United States with the exposés of the muckrakers.[35] Similar attacks later helped to undermine and overthrow the French Third Republic.[36]

[34] See, for example, Giovanni Maranini, "Stato di partiti, non partitocrazia," in *Studi politici*, VII (1960), 278–287.

[35] See, for example, Lincoln Steffens, *The Autobiography of Lincoln Steffens* (New York: Harcourt, Brace, 1931), Part III.

[36] See, for example, D. W. Brogan, *The Development of Modern France, 1870–1933* (London: Hamish Hamilton, 1940), Book X, chs. 6 and 7.

Elitist Theories

Other critics of parliament have attacked the basis of parliamentary democracy from the viewpoint of élitist theory. This belief divides society into two categories: leaders and followers. Harrington suggested that only about a third of a population could be considered as natural leaders; and that political power should be given to the better of these.[37] This theory was revived by a long series of nineteenth- and twentieth-century political theorists, who called these leaders bourgeoisie (Marx), *classe politica* (Mosca), élite (Pareto), chiselers (Howard Scott, the "technocrat"), the managers (Burnham), the rulers (Sereno), or the garrulous—as opposed to the gullible (an Australian wit cited by Crisp). Other common descriptions such as the few, the rich, the nobles, the clergy (that is, those who read and write), the haves, the insiders, the *furbi*, the oligarchs, the aristocrats, the master race, are not associated with a single author.

Gaetano Mosca applied the theory to parliamentary government, asserting that "in an election the majority is always necessarily completely passive and the choice of the deputy is imposed by a small organized minority." ". . . It is usually not the voters who elect the deputy, but the deputy who gets himself elected by the voters." [38]

---

[37] ". . . [T]wenty men (if they be not all *ideots,* perhaps if they be) can never come together, but there will be such difference in them, that about a *third* will be wiser, or at least *lesse* foolish than the rest. . . . Wherefore this can be no other than a naturall Aristocracy diffused by God through the whole body of mankind . . . for while the *six* discoursing and arguing one with another shew the eminence of their parts, the *fourteen* discover things they never thought on . . . wherefore in matters of common concernment, difficulty or danger, they hang upon their lips as *children* upon their fathers"—cited in Blitzer, *op. cit.,* p. 151. (The sentence order and spelling differ in the version of *Oceana* in *Ideal Commonwealth* [New York and London: Colonial Press, 1901], pp. 195 and 196.)

[38] Mosca, *Teorica,* ch. 5, sec. 2; ch. 6, sec. 2.

A generation later, Roberto Michels, a disciple of Mosca, developed his law of oligarchy, which states that hierarchy is endemic in organization and that the leaders of mass movements such as labor unions or political parties have a rapport with their followers not inherently different from the relations between other rulers and their subjects:

> It is organization which gives birth to the domination of the elected over the electors. . . . Who says organization says oligarchy. . . . Organization is, in fact, the source from which the conservative currents flow over the plain of democracy. . . . The social revolution would not effect any real modification of the internal structure of the mass. The socialists might conquer, but not socialism, which would perish in the moment of its adherents' triumph. We are tempted to speak of this process as a tragi-comedy in which the masses are content to devote all their energies to effecting a change of masters. All that is left to the workers is the honor of participating in government recruiting.[39]

Big Government

Another group of critics have decried parliament's inability to cope with the problems of big government, problems that they contend have arisen as a result of the changed social conditions and aspirations of the present century. The magnitude of gov-

[39] Robert Michels, *Zur Soziologie des Parteiwesens in der modernen Demokratie: Untersuchungen über die oligarchischen Tendenzen des Gruppenlebens* (Leipzig: 1910). Citation from English translation entitled *Political Parties* (New York: Collier Books, 1962), pp. 15, 62,, 354–355.

For a presentation and critique of Mosca's theory, see James H. Meisel, *The Myth of the Ruling Class* (Ann Arbor, Mich.: University of Michigan Press, 1958). For recent developments in élitist theory, see C. Wright Mills, *The Power Élite* (New York: Oxford University Press, 1956) (pessimistic from the liberal democratic point of view), and Renzo Sereno, *The Rulers* (Leiden: E. J. Brill, 1962).

ernment, the need for reliance on experts, the frequent speed and secrecy in decision-making have, they say, been detrimental to parliamentary power and prestige.

In 1929, Lord Chief Justice Gordon Hewart of Bury, in his book *The New Despotism,* warned of the encroachment of an expanded executive branch on legislative and judicial organs. He inveighed bitterly against the increased use of delegated legislation, which tended to make the administration both lawmaker and judge. Hewart's attack was from the viewpoint of the common law jurist, who rightly saw in the new balance between parliament and the executive a serious threat to the prestige of the judiciary and to their ability to perform adequately their traditional function of defending individual rights.

Lord Hewart's concern was not an isolated instance of this line of reasoning. His book attracted a deal of attention and a Royal Commission was appointed to investigate and report on the matter. The report, issued eight years later, substantiated the less exaggerated charges and considered them an inevitable consequence of social change.[40]

Nearly a quarter century after the appearance of Lord Hewart's book, parliament's decline and failure was described in a shocking manner by George William Keeton:

> Basically, the issues dividing the nation at the outbreak of the Civil War were two, and they are precisely the two which have provoked increasing concern at the present day. The first was the question whether the King possessed a legislative power, independent of Parliamentary control. The second was whether the . . . historic common laws of England . . . governed all causes and all men, or whether, on the contrary, the King, by virtue of the royal prerogative, had the power to create new courts dispensing "administrative justice." [41]

[40] "In truth, whether good or bad, the development of the practice is inevitable. It is a natural reflection, in the sphere of constitutional law, of changes in our ideas of government which have resulted in changes in our political, social, and economic ideas, and of changes in the circumstances of our lives . . ."—cited in Sir Ivor Jennings, *Parliament* (Cambridge: Cambridge University Press, 1957), pp. 477–478.

[41] *The Passing of Parliament* (London: Ernest Benn, Ltd., 1952), pp. 35–36.

Keeton's argument implies that the British have come full circle and stand now roughly where they were when they were forced to behead Charles I; the only difference is that the present tyrant is not the king but a many-headed hydra.

A less arresting but perhaps sounder statement on the British situation comes from Professor John P. Mackintosh:

> . . . Parliament does not now wield powers which can be said to amount to "control of the executive." Once a government is in office, Parliament and the party outside Parliament stand in the position of highly important pressure groups whose support must be retained and who therefore have direct and recognized avenues for approaching the Premier and his colleagues. . . . There is therefore a record of occasional adjustments to meet the views of the party stalwarts from the constituencies and a much larger number of cases where ministers take in the views of their back benchers in framing measures and adjust their schemes to suggestions and even pressure from their party committees. . . . But such influence is seldom exercised in the open in free debate and it fails to attract attention so that Parliament has tended to fall in public estimation a little further than its position as the leading source of political pressure in the country merits." [42]

Professor Stephen K. Bailey isolates four factors that he believes are responsible among them for much of the additional strain on parliamentary procedure that has become operative in the last half century.[43] They are (1) a condition of constant crisis; (2) the requirements of modern diplomacy and defense; (3) the growth of technology; and (4) the growth of bureaucracy (discussed above). Let us look briefly at the first three of these factors.

We have seen in Chapter 1 how in periods of crisis and change, *iurisdictio* gives way to *gubernaculum*. Parliament is a delib-

---

[42] John P. Mackintosh, *The British Cabinet* (London: Stevens & Sons, Ltd., 1962), pp. 503–504. For a more detailed analysis of the problem as it relates to Great Britain, see C. K. Allen, *Law and Orders* (London, Stevens & Sons, Ltd., 1956).

[43] In an address delivered in Washington, October 19, 1961, before the management interns of the United States government.

erative assembly; it is also a deliberate assembly and it is not at its best when it is forced to hurry. Thus, in the words of Bailey:

> In the repetitive convulsions of our era, is it any wonder that we have submitted to what Clinton Rossiter has called "Constitutional Dictatorship"—that we have sought comfort in the solemn singularity and emergency discretion of the Presidency? Is it any wonder that the Congress itself has sought such comfort? It was a Republican, not a Democratic Congressman, who said when the Emergency Banking Act of 1933 was submitted to vote in the Congress without so much as a legislative hearing, or even a printed bill:
>
> "Of course it is entirely out of the ordinary to pass legislation in this House that, as far as I know, is not even in print at the time it is offered. The House is burning down and the President of the United States says this is the way to put out the fire. . . . I am going to give the President of the United States his way today. He is the man responsible and we must follow his lead." [44]

Our increasing concern with diplomacy and defense also stacks the cards against the legislature and forces departures from ideally "democratic" procedures. Woodrow Wilson's maxim, "Open covenants openly arrived at," was surely one of the most irresponsible ever coined by a public leader. Diplomats need freedom and privacy and unity of direction in order to negotiate. There must be give-and-take, and a preestablished intransigence on the part of the general public or its representatives renders successful diplomacy virtually impossible.

Just as diplomacy requires secrecy and unity of direction, so national defense is based on secret information, secret preparation, and swift decisions. When the Founding Fathers delegated to congress the power to declare war, they obviously did not have an atomic war in mind; and today that constitutional provision is as effectively dead as if it had been formally repealed. For valid security reasons, parliaments not only cannot control foreign policy; at times, they cannot even be informed of that policy.

[44] *Ibid.*

During the Munich and the Suez crises, the British parliament and even the cabinet were kept in the dark; policy was determined by prime ministers Chamberlain and Eden after consultation with a handful of trusted political allies.[45] President Kennedy ordered preparations for and actually attempted the invasion of Cuba via the Bay of Pigs in 1961, taking only a few key congressmen into his confidence. Though one may regret the decisions, in this case no one could suggest that the whole matter should have been thrashed out in congress.

Even if international tensions were miraculously to decrease—if lions, bears, eagles, and dragons should learn to live in peace with each other and with the other smaller animals—parliaments would still be faced with problems quite alien to those imagined by early liberal democratic philosophers. The growth of science and technology poses policy decisions that the average deputy is not prepared to comprehend. Moreover, the economic interests that seek government subsidies in the name of aerospace projects and military preparedness form one of the most formidable pressure groups with which a parliament has ever been faced. By now, parliaments have lost the effective use of the power of the purse by default, because deputies on the whole understand neither the budget nor fiscal policy. The Bundesrat's rejection of the German budget in 1963, and the Italian rejection of a single item in the budget in 1964 and 1965, are among the few instances in postwar Europe of an action traditionally assumed to be a normal parliamentary check. The American congress is an exception in that it still exercises its budgetary prerogatives, but it is doubtful that congressional amendments, which generally cater to minority interests, improve upon the coordinated executive budget. The same may be said in general for the exercise of budgetary control by the American state legislatures.

The very size of modern government leaves the deputy with a sense of bewilderment and inadequacy. There are not enough hours in a day for him to keep informed of currently important matters. He is dependent on the advice and counsel of the

[45] Mackintosh, *op. cit.,* p. 436.

bureaucrat and most of the time he must accept or reject that advice blindly. The specialist, who theoretically should be on tap, is in effect on top. Legislative power is delegated to the specialists. Moreover, because of the enormity of the load, parliament must relinquish any close and constant control over the government.

In this chapter, parliament has stood as the accused. The brief for the prosecution here presented is formidable. It will be the task of the final chapter to present the case for the defense.

6.

THE TRADITIONAL ROLE OF PARLIAMENT AND THE LEGISLATIVE FUNCTION:

A Case of Mistaken Identity and Misjudged Potential

Parliament and the General Will

However widespread the criticisms of parliament may be, however tellingly they may strike at the heart of the parliamentary system, however inexorably they may seem to support a prognosis of the inevitable and rapid demise of that body, they have been considerably belied by the facts. The sentence of doom that can logically be derived from the criticisms has never materialized. Liberal democracy as a political philosophy or a political process may not have been as readily transplantable as its more optimistic propagandists had assumed, but in the western world where it took root a century or more ago, it remains prestigious as a system of values and functional as a system of government. It is no magic wand that can effortlessly summon utopia, but the vast majority of westerners who think and care about such things are devoted to it; while many of those who neither think nor care react favorably to the platitudes in which the conventional wisdom has obfuscated its essence. There are some dozen countries in the world in which liberal democracy can boast a century or more of popular and successful operation. In each case, one of the major institutions involved has been parliament. Parliament, then, in spite of the many justified and basic criticisms to which it has been subjected, is a common factor in the governmental process of all firmly established liberal democracies.

The quasi paradox that develops in surveying the criticisms of parliament on the one hand, and the generally admitted accomplishments of liberal democracy on the other can, I believe, be explained in the following manner.[1] The philosophers of liberal democracy were not social scientists. They worked in the realm of ideas and values and benefited from varying degrees of practical experience with politics, but they had little understanding of the nature of social groups. The modern study of society on a quasi-scientific basis first made headway in France in the nineteenth century, after many of the great philosophers of liberal democracy were already entombed. It opened a new window on social life, one that often gives a clearer view and better understanding of social behavior.

Sociologically, we divide human and—to the extent appropriate—animal activity into broad, mutually exclusive categories, distinguishing conceptually between activities affecting things and those affecting other people. Activities affecting things have to do with their location, transformation, transportation, and consumption. To accomplish these tasks, man originally relied on his physical strength and dexterity. But possessing also an intellect, man soon learned that he could increase the efficacy of his strength and dexterity by the use of tools. The knife, the ax, the bow and arrow, and later the wheel and the axle, are among man's early and most important tools.

A greater control of man's physical environment resulted from

[1] For the material discussed in the following pages, see, among others, Santi Romano, *L'ordinamento giuridico* (Pisa, 1918) (2d ed., Florence: Sansoni, 1945); René Maunier, *Introduction à la sociologie* (Paris: Félix Alcan, 1929); A. R. Radcliffe Brown, "Sanctions, social," in *Encyclopedia of the Social Sciences* (New York: The Macmillan Company, 1934), Vol. XIII; A. R. Radcliffe Brown, *A Natural Science of Society* (New York: The Free Press of Glencoe, 1954); and John Clarke Adams, "Diritto e società nell'ordine naturale e nell'ordine giuridico," in *Scritti giuridici in memoria di Piero Calamandrei* (Padua: CEDAM, 1958), Vol. I, pp. 41–56.

the invention of the machine. Where the tool merely increases the effectiveness of his physical force and skill, the machine permits him to exploit a force not his own. Slaves and animals were indubitably the first machines. The more recent rapid development of machines brought about the Industrial Revolution and the spectacular increase in man's control of his physical environment.

A similar development has occurred in man's relation to his social environment. Here again three levels of control can be distinguished. The primitive level is that of spontaneous social groups, where control is exercised through the diffuse sanctions of approval or condemnation expressed by significant numbers of group members as a reaction to socially significant behavior. Spontaneous reactions to behavior, however, are as exhausting to the psyche as manual labor is to the physical body, and man has thus been encouraged by necessity to devise substitutes. One substitute, the rite, is analogous to the tool. It is a formalized and symbolic expression of a reaction that is normally not experienced in full internally. This device makes possible socially useful external behavior at a greatly minimized expenditure of psychic (and intellectual) energy.

But spontaneous sanctions and ritual expressions are not sufficient to maintain the many thousands of social groups with which modern man has surrounded himself. In order to sustain these groups, he invented something that would serve him in the world of social relations for roughly the purpose served in the economic world by the machine. This invention was the institution. An institution is an artifact of man's mind, a creature of law. It is composed of organs, organization, and personnel. States, churches, fraternities, corporations, clubs, universities, and any other formal group organization are all institutions in this sense. Animals have considerable experience with spontaneous groups; they appear to have rites, but there is no evidence that they have institutions. On the other hand, institutions are essential to the development of social systems that resemble ours.

Members of spontaneous groups set up institutions and empower them to act in the name of the group and for the furtherance of its interests. In doing so they serve two ends. In the first place, spontaneous groups are supported only by the sporadic attention of their members, for no group (or no series of groups, for that matter) represents the whole man. With the creation of the institution group, interests are permanently represented even during the slack periods when the attention of the group members is elsewhere. And in the second place, a properly functioning institution can relieve the individual members of the spontaneous group it serves of the responsibility for considering and reacting to all instances of socially significant behavior. This it does by substituting for the spontaneous (diffuse) sanctions of the parent group its own organized (that is, legal) sanctions. Like the diffuse sanctions, the legal sanctions may be positive (for example, knighthood, congressional medals, Legion of Honor) or negative (for example, fines or imprisonment).

Most spontaneous groups except the smallest and the shortest lived are reinforced by an apposite institution. A major exception is the amorphous group of neighborhood children (not, of course, the organized groups of teen-age delinquents). Here there is no institutionalization of authority: the common goals of the group are achieved, and the necessary conformity imposed, by the spontaneous efforts of the members, who are willing to devote a large amount of their attention and energy to these ends.

Two aspects of institutions are of particular interest to us here.

First, institutions do not always serve the interest of the group of which they are ostensibly the formal organization. An institution requires people to run it, and there is a tendency for officers of institutions to serve their own group interests or the interests of some other subgroup rather than those of the group for the protection of whose interests the institution was formally established. When this happens we have what Aristotle calls a bad state, that is, one in which the ruling group rules in the interest of a part rather than the whole of the polity. Any institution that in fact represents a social group other than the totality of the persons and interests it was established to represent is acting tyrannically toward the persons it fails to represent. This is a potential weakness of a liberal democratic parliament as well as of any other type of institution, and the tendency to a corruption of this kind is endemic in all institutions.

Secondly—and it is here that we run into major difficulties with the democratic theorists—the function of an institution is not so much to express the will of the members of the spontaneous social group it represents as to supply an ersatz will for the will that the spontaneous group has not formulated. So long as the spontaneous group has the time and energy to formulate and express a will, there is no need for an institution. It is when this will, essential for the realization of group interests, is lacking that it becomes necessary to establish an institution.

The political theorists of democracy had their minds set on the development of a procedure whereby *vox populi* could be converted into *lex*. Parliament was a prestigious organ of government with which they were familiar; it was a traditional bulwark against executive overbearance in those states that the democratic theorists particularly admired. No wonder they proposed making parliament a body more nearly representative of all the people and conferring on it the legislative power.

The basic weakness of parliament as a legislative body is not its inability to reflect the will of the people. Members of parliament, having experienced the honor of being elected to public office, will usually go to considerable lengths to be reelected. Such persons are quite sensitive to public opinion; they seldom misjudge and only rarely disregard a clear mandate from the people. Politicians may be willing to deceive the people, to divert them from following their best interests by plying them with red herrings, scapegoats, and assorted misinformation and by pandering to their intemperate passions. But no politician dares make a practice of flaunting the conscious, expressed wishes of the electorate. In a democratic system, with regular and honest elections, it is clear to the most obtuse seeker of elective office that the electors are the ultimate masters whenever they determine to assert their authority.[2] Any state, however tyrannically it is organized, any institution will cease to exist if it no longer receives

[2] It may take the voters some time to persuade parliament that they are in earnest, particularly if the selfish interests of the legislators are at stake. For an example of failure to heed the general will, see Gordon E. Baker, *The Politics of Reapportionment in Washington State* (New York: McGraw-Hill Book Co., 1960).

the positive support of the people, for this support is to institutions what oxygen is to animals and the sun to plants. The French and Russian revolutions give dramatic evidence of the catastrophic consequences that occur when states lose popular support. The present preoccupation with political alienation attests to our concern over the effects of what might be called incipient or partial institutional asphyxiation.

If one maintains, however (as this writer does), that so long as the spontaneous group is able to express its wishes and accomplish its ends through formulations and continued reiterations of its will, there is actually little need to institutionalize sanctions; then only when the complexities of the desired social controls call for expenditure in psychic and intellectual energy beyond the ability of the members of the spontaneous group does the constitution of a legal order become imperative. Thus the legislative function is not primarily the faithful reflection of the people's will, but rather the determination of an ersatz will for that preponderance of instances in which the voice of the people has not been heard. "Public opinion," A. Lawrence Lowell is quoted as having said, "is not the opinion of the majority . . . it is the opinion to which the majority will yield or conform, and that ungrudgingly." [3] Under these conditions it is true that parliament has had difficulty in performing the legislative function, that it has failed to produce the results expected of it by the democratic theorists. Parliament can process *vox populi* and transform it into legislation; it is not adept at fabricating single-handedly an ersatz *vox populi*. This process, distinctly different from parliament's traditional functions, can only be carried out successfully by a collaboration between parliament and the ex-

[3] Cited in William Starr Myers, "The Meaning of Democracy," *Annals of the American Academy of Political and Social Science,* CLXIX (1933), 47. James Bryce expressed the same feeling in the following words: "The obvious weakness of government by opinion is the difficulty of ascertaining it . . . like other valuable articles genuine opinion is surrounded by counterfeit"— *The American Commonwealth* (New York: The Macmillan Company, 1899), ch. 86, para. 1. John F. Kennedy was also in agreement: "I rarely know what the great majority of voters feel"—*Profiles in Courage* (New York: Harper & Row, 1955), p. 18.

ecutive-administrative branch of government: a collaboration that has been made difficult by those theorists—and they include many of the great names of liberal democratic thought—who subscribed to the doctrine of the separation of powers and therefore assigned the legislative function exclusively or almost exclusively to parliament.

The Separation of Powers

This doctrine, as developed by Montesquieu, was intended as a safeguard against the tyranny that it was claimed would result from the concentration of power in one man or body of men. Montesquieu stated his case as follows:

> . . . if there were no monarch and . . . [if] the executive power were given to a certain number of persons taken from the legislative body, there would be no more liberty, because the two powers would be joined; as the same persons would have or would be able to have a share in both.[4]

Rousseau was even more adamant on this point, although there is some inconsistency in his writing on the subject between what he says in *Du contrat social* (1762) and in *Considérations sur le gouvernement de Pologne* (1782). In the former work, he held that the legislative function belongs to the whole community and cannot be delegated even to representatives. Application of the general will is the function of an appointed commission charged with implementation. He called this commission the executive. Rousseau's use of the terms "legislative" and "executive" in *Du contrat social,* however, did not correspond with general practice. In the *Contrat social* the legislative function was virtually limited to matters of constitutional importance, and the executive func-

[4] Charles Louis de Secondat, Baron de la Brède et de Montesquieu, *De l'esprit des lois* (Geneva, 1748).

tion included most of what many other writers refer to as the combined legislative, executive, and judicial functions of government. In his book on Poland, however, he seems to use these terms in a more conventional manner while still insisting on complete separation.[5]

To the degree that the doctrine has been construed as the separation of power, rather than of powers, and has admitted checks and balances—and this has usually been the case *de facto* and *de iure*—it has been a useful but not entirely effective impediment to tyranny. Every attempt to set up airtight compartments separating powers or functions of government on the basis of theoretical concepts has created a totally unworkable system, however, for the executive has played a major role in legislation in all periods. The *consilium principis* of Rome,[6] the *curia regis* of the British kings and its European counterparts, the kings and emperors themselves, the princes, the presidents, the prime ministers, and the trusted experienced career administrators (the British permanent undersecretaries, their historical antecedents, and their foreign counterparts) have always played and must always play a dominant role in the formation of policy and consequently in legislation.

Although Montesquieu wrote his *De l'esprit des lois* believing, or perhaps pretending, that he was describing the English system of government, the separation of powers he advocated has never existed in England. James Madison, defending the English constitution in *The Federalist,* wrote that on "the slightest view of the British Constitution we must perceive that the legislative, executive, and judiciary departments are by no means totally separate and distinct from each other" and that if "we look into

[5] See M. J. C. Vile, *Constitutionalism and the Separation of Powers* (London: Oxford University Press, 1967), chs. VII, IX, and particularly pp. 177–183. See also Frank Marini, "Popular Sovereignty but Representative Government: The Other Rousseau," *Midwest Journal of Political Science,* XI (1967), 451–470. For a lucid, extreme, but far less influential statement of the doctrine of a complete separation of powers, see John Taylor of Caroline, *An Inquiry into the Principles and Policy of the Government of the United States* (Fredericksburg, 1814).

[6] See J. A. Crook, *Consilium principis* (Cambridge: Cambridge University Press, 1955), particularly pp. 115–128.

the constitutions of the several States, we find that . . . there is
not a single instance in which the several departments of power
have been kept absolutely separate and distinct." [7] Walter Bagehot, writing almost a century later, held that the secret of the
English constitution "was the close union, the nearly complete
fusion, of executive and legislative powers." [8] A distinguished
New Zealand jurist has recently put the same conclusion fe-
licitously:

> "Be it enacted by the Queen's most excellent Majesty, by and
> with the consent of the Lords Spiritual and Temporal, and Com-
> mons in this present Parliament assembled." So read and reads
> the preamble to a British statute. What does it signify?
> The formula says that, traditionally, legislation is enacted by
> the Crown, or in effect, ministers, with the advice and consent
> of Parliament. The legislative predominance of Cabinet is not
> some modern corruption of the constitution, but the traditional
> system, a system that was to some extent in abeyance during the
> ninteenth century. The legislative independence of private
> members of Parliament in the nineteenth century was not a
> time-honored feature of Parliament, but an aberration that be-
> devilled politics with local questions. The legislative system has
> now been restored to its earlier form. As M. L. S. Amery said,
> "The British constitution is not so much flexible as elastic." [9]

Even in Italy, where parliament still wields more power than in
other parliamentary systems, a leading jurist asserts that

> It is merely a fiction to say that parliament performs the legisla-
> tive function. . . . There is a single organ, the government,
> responsible for both administration and legislation, under the
> watchful eye of another organ, parliament, which supervises
> administration and legislation with the same intensity.[10]

[7] (1787–88), No. 47.

[8] *The English Constitution,* 1867.

[9] K. J. Scott, *The New Zealand Constitution* (London: Oxford University
Press, 1962), p. 55.

[10] Giorgio Balladore Pallieri, "Appunti sulla divisione dei poteri nella
vigente costituzione italiana," *Rivista trimestrale di diritto pubblico,* II
(1952), 811–830 at 811.

A closely related but equally unfounded shibboleth of the conventional wisdom has held that there is a dichotomy of policy formation and administration.[11] It is no longer necessary to belabor the point that this dichotomy exists only on the conceptual plane. Students of public administration agree that, in practice, policymaking and execution, which closely resemble the jurist's categories of legislation and execution, are so intricately intertwined that on examination they appear to be, not distinct functions, but merely different aspects of the same activity. Thus the legislative process, which is the process that determines not all but much of major policy, cannot be confined to a single organ of the state but must operate within all organs exercising prime authority. The constitution may require a series of formal procedures within parliament in order to validate the enactment of law; but these are in a sense rituals that can neither contain nor control all the forces the interplay among which determines policy. Except in periods of anarchy or near anarchy, however, political decisions are channeled through these prescribed procedures and the real power struggle takes place to some degree within the prescribed process.[12]

Yet, in spite of conclusive evidence to the contrary,[13] the myth of the separation of powers, with its emphasis on representative assemblies as the sole lawmaking bodies, has continued to hold sway. This myth is further strengthened by the esteem traditionally attached in democratic countries to the legislature as the representative of the people—in contrast to the executive, whose fate was to inherit the suspicion the people had of the

[11] See, for example, Frank J. Goodnow, *Politics and Administration, A Study in Government* (New York: The Macmillan Company, 1900).

[12] See, for example, Frank Sarouf, "Extra-Legal Parties in Wisconsin," *American Political Science Review*, XLIX (1954), 692–704.

[13] The writing in this field is voluminous. Other than the material cited, the following books and articles are provocative: Gabriel A. Almond and G. Bingham Powell, Jr., *Comparative Politics: A Developmental Approach* (Boston: Little, Brown & Co., 1966), ch. VI; Karl Loewenstein, "The Balance between Legislative and Executive Power: A Study in Comparative Constitutional Law," *University of Chicago Law Review*, V (1938), 566–608 at 573; and Filippo Bassi, "Il principio della separazione dei poteri," *Rivista trimestrale di diritto pubblico*, XV (1965), 17–113.

ruling monarch. A good deal of what may be called the crisis of
parliamentary government in modern democracies may be due
to the impact this myth has had on our political institutions and
procedures.

There have, nonetheless, been acute observers of the legislative
process over the centuries who have ascribed to parliament a
function within this process more reasonable and more natural,
in that it is more consonant with parliament's activities and pro-
clivities. Thus James Harrington emphasized the importance of
checks and balances between the various powers rather than a
concept of intrinsic separation of functions. He held that the
legislative function was to be *shared* between a body of experts
that would propose and a more representative assembly that
would dispose. John Stuart Mill gave a similar view in his
Representative Government (1860). He assigned the role of the
actual preparation of legislation to the selected, skilled few,
either elected for five-year terms by the legislature or appointed
for life like peers, reserving to the people (or rather, some of
them) through their representatives the role of accepting or re-
jecting the legislative proposals so prepared.[14]

Conclusion

It is in the performance of the legislative function, so far removed from those historically associated with parliament, that
the major failures of liberal democratic parliaments are found.
Thus the most general and most telling accusations against parliament have been directed at the difficulties it has experienced
in carrying out a task it was never equipped to undertake. With
this in mind, we are forced to reexamine the functioning of parliament and to ascertain its actual role in the legislative process.

Given a society in which the common man demands protection
and material aid from the state in ever-increasing degree, given

[14] Chapter 4.

a social structure so complex that the citizen is quite unable to have an informed opinion on the majority of issues pertinent to his well-being, policy must be made for him. And policy frequently means legislation. Somewhere in the formal legislative process there must be an opportunity for all interested groups to be heard, whether it be to inform the lawmakers of the supposed effect any bill under consideration will have on them, to offer counterproposals and amendments, or to initiate consideration of a matter not then under scrutiny. When no other organ offers this guarantee, parliament must do it.

The traditional and the natural function of parliament is that of defender of the people. As such, it must be able to hear and to be heard in the legislative process; it must be able to amend or reject proposals inimical to the general welfare, and to initiate bills *pro bono publico* in those cases where others fail to act. It is not necessary that parliament monopolize the role of the defender of the public in the legislative process. In many cases, this role can be performed successfully only by the cooperation of divers bodies. In a liberal democracy, however, there must be a formally constituted organ through which the will of the people may be expressed authoritatively whenever the people resolve to express their will.

It has been said that a people has the government it deserves. A people also has the parliament it deserves. A determined people means a determined parliament; a parliament with popular support effects its will without bloodshed or revolution. In the last resort, the availability of such an organ is the essential feature of liberal democracy that distinguishes this form of government from all other types. Only the most prejudiced of observers would disagree with the sentiment attributed to Count Cavour: "The worst chamber is better than the best antechamber."

INDEX OF AUTHORS CITED

SUBJECT INDEX